THE COMPLETE GUIDE TO

KITCHEN DESIGN

With

COOKING IN MIND

Donald E. Silvers, CKD
CERTIFIED KITCHEN DESIGNER

Illustrations by John Reister

NMI Publishers

Tarzana, California

Third Printing

Published by
NMI Publishers
18345 Ventura Boulevard,
Suite 314
Tarzana, CA 91356

Illustrations by John Reister

Library of Congress Catalog Number: 93-87773

ISNB: 0-932767-04-4

Printed in the United States of America

ACKNOWLEDGMENTS

I would like to thank the following people:

Jerry Zerg, for encouraging me to write.

B. Leslie Hart, for publishing my first article.

Carol Lamkins, Mike Goldberg, Don O'Connor,
David Andrews, my daughter Michelle and cousins
Essie and Diane, for the first read-through
of this book and their most thoughtful comments.

Josh Silvers, my son, who keeps me focused on the cooking process.

John Avram, for teaching me about kitchen cabinets.

NKBA dealers, for implementing my designs.
Bob Sellinger, for always responding to my frenetic phone calls,
and giving me the information I needed.

Joe Lavitt, for the title of the book.

Susan Volpe, for her patience and energy in helping me put the book together.

My editors, Louise Damberg and Carol Crotta,
for their quest to make this book the best it can be.

John Reister, for his wonderful illustrations.

My wife, Sally, who created the environment for this book to happen.

Special thanks to my publisher, Jerry Newmark, for
his encouragement and guidance throughout this entire project.

CONTENTS

INTRODUCTION • 1
Designing for the Cook • 1
How Bad Design Can Affect Your Life in the Kitchen • 2
Silvers' Law of Kitchen Design • 3

Chapter 1 **DESIGN BASICS** • 7
Your Kitchen as Your Workshop • 7
Breaking Free of the Kitchen Triangle • 8
Appliances Drive the Design • 8
The Subsystem Approach • 10

Chapter 2 **STORAGE SUBSYSTEMS** • 17
Cabinetry Dry Storage • 17
    Your options • 18
        Stock modular • 18
        Semi-custom modular • 18
        Custom modular • 18
        Custom millwork • 20
    Choosing cabinetry • 20
        Materials and finishes • 23
Refrigeration Cold Storage • 23

Chapter 3 **FOOD PREPARATION SUBSYSTEMS** • 27
Counters • 27
    The 30-in.-deep counter • 28
    Counter surfaces • 28
        Post-formed and custom laminates • 28
        Ceramic kitchen tile • 28
        Wood • 30
        Solid surfaces • 30
        Granite • 30
Small Appliances • 30
The Prep Sink and Other Prep Areas • 31

Chapter 4   **COOKING SUBSYSTEMS • 30**

Cooktops • 35

Your options • 37

Gas • 37

Electric • 38

Magnetic induction • 38

Halogen • 39

Other Cooking Surfaces and Equipment • 39

Your options • 39

Charbroilers • 39

Griddles • 41

Hoods/ventilation systems • 41

Ovens • 43

Your options • 43

Electric radiant • 43

Convection • 43

Microwave • 45

Convection/microwave • 46

Ranges • 47

Chapter 5   **CLEAN-UP SUBSYSTEMS • 51**

Sinks • 51

Your options • 53

Faucets • 53

Water-processing systems • 54

Disposals • 54

Dishwashers • 54

Trash Compactors • 55

Chapter 6   **TWO CRITICAL DESIGN ELEMENTS FROM FLOOR TO CEILING • 59**

Flooring • 59

Your options • 59

Vinyl sheet and custom vinyl • 59

Hardwood • 59

Designer woods • 59

Ceramic tile • 59

Natural stone • 60

Lighting • 60

Chapter 7   **THE TOOLS OF THE TRADE** • 63

Pots and Pans • 63

    Materials • 64

        Stainless steel • 64

        Cast iron • 64

        Glass • 64

        Aluminum • 65

        Copper • 65

        Non-stick • 66

Knives • 66

Chapter 8   **WORKING WITH A DESIGNER** • 71

The Full-Service Designer • 72

How a Design Fee Is Calculated • 74

Appendix   **YOUR KITCHEN QUESTIONNAIRE** • 82

INTRODUCTION

You are about to embark on one of the most daunting experiences you'll ever have as a homeowner: designing (or redesigning) your kitchen. No wonder you're apprehensive. You're no expert in kitchen design. You feel as though you're at the mercy of your designer, your architect, your contractor, your cabinetmaker. Adding to this stress is the fact you're about to invest a considerable amount of money and you will have to live with the results. You pray you will get a kitchen that not only looks good but works well.

Any number of books and magazines on the market today can tell you how to put together an attractive kitchen. Aesthetics are important, of course, but for people who cook, aesthetics are only half the story. This book tells the other half—how to design your kitchen for cooking.

Designing for the Cook

When people tell me, "I hate to cook," I've learned from experience many really are saying, "I hate to cook in my kitchen." After you've read this book, and the work is done, I want you to be able to say, "I love to cook in my kitchen." After all the money and effort, you deserve a beautiful kitchen that is also a joy to work in.

It begins with the designer. One of the most prevalent misconceptions I hear is that you don't need to understand the process of cooking to design a proper kitchen. Rarely, if ever, is a designer asked if he or she knows how to cook. And yet, the kitchen is a complex space—so complex, in fact, that it deserves the services of a specialist. The problem is, most people have spent years adjusting and re-adjusting themselves and their recipes to accommodate their kitchen's poor design. They lose sight of the potential a well-designed kitchen offers. Years ago, a restaurant owner asked me to design his kitchen. After spending many weeks conferring with each employee, and working at every station myself, I presented my design. Everyone loved it except the executive chef. He couldn't tell me exactly what was wrong. He simply said it didn't look right. I understood what was wrong.

Here was a man who had spent his entire 30-year career in this kitchen, working his way up from dishwasher to executive chef. He knew every nook and cranny. He felt comfortable in that environment. The changes I proposed had scared him. I asked if I could work next to him for the next few hours, to show him why I had designed the way I had. He agreed. I taped the new plan to the kitchen hood and we went at it.

As I explained to him while we worked, his kitchen actually hampered his ability to cook. The restaurant did a big business in steaks, but his refrigerator sat 20 feet from the charbroiler. The salad prep table was located right in the middle of the hot cooking area. The road to the dishwashing area wound through the cooking zone. What I proposed to do, I told him, was to consolidate his equipment, and reconfigure the relationship of each one to the other.

I wanted to put in a modular charbroiler, and sit it atop a lowboy refrigerator with drawers that could hold—what else?—steaks. I rearranged the lineup to place the cooktop and tilting fry-pan stations together, which had previously been separated by the deep-fat fryers. To this lineup I added another essential: a rolling steam table with a tall electric holding oven that could house several prime rib slabs, another restaurant specialty. Before, the holding oven was 20 to 25 feet away, and could only house one prime rib at a time. I also explained to the chef how I would reposition the salad table to a cooler side of the room, and reroute the busboys with their trays of dirty dishes.

Two hours later, and with a big grin, the chef pronounced the plan great. He thanked me for showing him that, because of the kitchen's existing design, an hour's worth of work was taking him two hours to accomplish.

Most of us are like that chef. We spend our lives in kitchens that are familiar and comfortable, yet waste a good bit of our time with their inefficiency. The process of designing a kitchen must go hand in hand with a thorough understanding of the process of cooking. Only then can you achieve a kitchen that is a pleasure to cook in, and that cooks well.

How Bad Design Can Affect Your Life in the Kitchen

The best example I can give of how the design of your kitchen can affect your life there is by way of a recipe. You've decided to throw a dinner party for eight. The entree you've chosen to prepare is mango chutney chicken. The recipe reads as follows:

8 chicken breasts (skinned and trimmed)

flour for dredging chicken

1/2 cup dry white wine

2 oz. orange liqueur

16 oz. mango chutney

(since chutney consistencies vary, you want to have extra on hand)

Wine or chicken stock (approx. 2 to 3 cups)

Pepper to taste

Preheat oven to 425 degrees. Cover the bottom of a 13-in. frying pan with a thin layer of avocado oil, and heat over a high flame until the oil is very hot. Dredge the breasts in flour, place in pan and fry over the high flame until browned on one side. Turn the breasts over and lower the heat. Add the wine and simmer until the liquid is reduced by half. Add the liqueur and ignite, agitating the pan as the alcohol burns off. Again reduce the liquid by half. Continue simmering the breasts until they are two-thirds cooked. Remove from frying pan and place on an oven rack set in a broiler pan. Pour mango chutney into frying pan and heat over a low flame, adding wine or chicken stock as needed to achieve a medium consistency (keep in mind that the flour residue will thicken the sauce; it should be just thick enough to stay on the breast). When the sauce is heated thoroughly, ladle a small amount over each breast, keeping the remainder warm, to spoon over the chicken before serving. Pour either the remaining wine or chicken stock (or water, in a pinch) in the bottom of the broiler pan to prevent the breasts from drying out. Reduce oven heat to 375 degrees (oven heat diminishes about one degree per second when the door is open, which is why you always want to preheat your oven about 50 degrees higher than the recommended cooking temperature) and bake breasts for 15 minutes. Place on a warm platter, spoon the remaining sauce over the top, and serve.

Now that you've read the recipe, you realize you can't make the dish in your kitchen exactly the way it is written. If you have the average stove, your burners are simply too small to properly heat a 13-in. frying pan. You might toy with the idea of using three separate pans to accommodate all the breasts, but give it up because the burners are too close together. You might consider frying the breasts in three separate batches, but that plan seems like too much work, and the breasts might dry out. The only other way is to use the oven. Now the process has to change. The chicken breasts must be raw when placed on the oven rack. You must spoon the sauce over them, but it, too, is altered. There are no pan drippings in it now, so it has lost a good bit of flavor, and it is thinner, since there is no flour to thicken it. You need to bake the breasts for 25 to 30 minutes. Sounds simple, maybe easier? You're right—but the chicken doesn't taste as good. Pan frying gives the flour-dredged chicken a crunchy surface, while keeping the breasts tender and soft on the inside. The textured surface also helps hold the sauce in place. In addition, the chicken breasts have a far more beautiful color when pan fried, thanks to the liqueur's glazing effect.

For anyone who cares about cooking, and about eating well, these differences in appearance, taste, texture and smell are painfully apparent. I don't mean to suggest this is the only way to cook. I do believe, however, that you should have this option. Your kitchen should be filled with options and, most important, should respond to your specific needs.

Silvers' Law of Kitchen Design

How do you get the kitchen you want? By beginning to explore your needs and desires. By asking yourself, first, and then your designer, a variety of questions. What kind of questions am I talking about? They deal with the basics:

- What size kitchen do I need and want?
- How many people do I cook for daily?
- How many people do I want to cook for on an informal basis? On a formal basis?
- Will my kitchen work in tandem with the number of people my dining room seats?
- What kind of appliances do I want? Do I need?
- Do I want to make structural changes?
- Do I want the kitchen to open to other rooms?
- Do I want more windows or other sources of natural light?
- Am I happy with the existing lighting?

- Do I want more or less counter and/or storage space?
- What style of decor do I prefer? And what materials does it require?
- Is my kitchen in keeping with the size of my house?
- How do I prioritize my budget?

Only when you've started to consider these issues can you begin to communicate your needs successfully to your designer. Twenty-five years ago, as food director for a large charity organization, I was forced to learn the basic principles of kitchen design. I was responsible for creating 4,000 to 6,000 meals per day in a kitchen designed to generate 500 meals. To make matters even more difficult, during my first two years there, 90 percent of the food was donated on a daily basis, so a planned menu was impossible. I was in serious trouble.

Many architects contacted by the organization volunteered their help. I received more than a dozen plans to redesign the kitchen. Despite having answered hundreds of questions put to me by the architects, none of the proposals seemed adequate. It became clear to me that, since none of the architects cooked, none of them actually understood how to make this kitchen work. As I rejected one plan after another, they finally threw up their hands in despair. Finally, the organization's director told me to design the kitchen myself. I was petrified. "I'm not a designer, I'm a chef!" I told him. "You know what you want and what you don't want," he replied.

Fortunate for me, the noted architect/philosopher Buckminster Fuller happened to be visiting. The director asked him to see me. "Bucky" found me knee-deep in a kitchen brimming with stacked boxes, crates and bags. As we stood in the last available two square feet of empty space, I explained my dilemma to him. He responded by asking me a question: "How do you take space and make it usable for small or large numbers of people?" He began to talk about how a space flows, and on how many levels it can flow. Since there obviously was no room to expand horizontally, he started me thinking about expanding vertically. The two floors below the kitchen lay empty and unused. The bottom I decided to turn into cold storage space for low-frequency items. The floor just below the kitchen opened to the street. I decided to turn that into the fresh food storage and prep area, and installed a conveyor setup that allowed crates to be rolled into the kitchen from the sidewalk outside.

Essentially, Bucky taught me to break down functions in the kitchen, give those functions the necessary space, and make sure those spaces worked not only on their own, but in relation to one another. The advice has served me well not only as a chef but as a designer. It has helped me to develop a principle of kitchen design that I've used ever since. Call it "Silvers' Law":

A functional kitchen has the ability to take a given space
and expand or compress the capacity of that space
so it can respond to a given need at a given time.

In the following pages, I endeavor to reduce a complex process to its simple components, in order to help you gain a kitchen that is as functional as it is beautiful. I have purposely not mentioned brand names. It doesn't matter who makes a product as long as it satisfies your needs. To know if it does, you must understand the product's structure, what it will or will not do, and how it will fit in your kitchen and the life you lead there.

What you want is a kitchen that is beautiful—and that you can cook in beautifully. It's not the impossible dream.

Notes

Chapter 1

DESIGN BASICS

I like to say that your bedroom may be the most private intimate room in your house, but the kitchen is the most public intimate room. An intimate environment is one that allows you to have a heart-to-heart talk with someone—a place where you can spend quality time with another individual. More often than not, that experience happens in the kitchen. Everything about that room—color, texture, overall atmosphere—should be inviting. Comfort is the key, and comfort comes from a number of elements. First of all, does it appeal to your senses? Do you feel good just being in the room? But comfort also comes from feeling good when you're working there, by having everything you need close at hand when you need it.

Simple concepts, right? The complexity comes from the wide array of activities a kitchen plays host to. A kitchen has to work well from the morning's first cup of coffee to the 2 a.m. refrigerator raid. It must adapt to the unique demands each activity makes on the space, whether that activity be accommodating the perpetual motion of children before, during and after meal preparation, creating a soothing haven for an afternoon cup of tea with a close friend, or graciously hosting family and guests for a meal.

Real comfort comes not just from pretty, comfortable surroundings, but from a solid, functional foundation. Comfort is knowing you can create a dinner for one or 20, with ease.

Any kitchen worth its salt should function, and feel, like a well-designed workshop. It should offer intelligent traffic flow patterns, a smartly organized layout and all the appropriate tools. The best kitchens marry workshop efficiency to a warm, personal, attractive environment. When any of these elements is missing, the kitchen ceases to be comfortable and cooking becomes just plain hard work.

Your Kitchen as Your Workshop

If you start thinking about your kitchen as a workshop, you immediately begin to make new demands on its design. First and foremost, it must be utilitarian. It must be designed to allow you to accomplish specific tasks as simply and quickly as possible. For example, one kitchen I worked on made it a chore just to have a bowl of cereal. The cereal was 22 feet away from the refrigerator, and the silverware 10 feet in yet another direction. In your kitchen, you should be able to bake a souffle as easily as you toss a salad or create a wonderful sauce. It also should be flexible enough to accommodate a variety of work demands and uses throughout the day and night.

In a workshop kitchen, tools and appliances should be accessible. The more equipment that is tucked away, the more time it takes to set up, and the more difficult it is to get to work. I know that some people prefer appliance "garages," or enclosed countertop cabinets that hide appliances until they are called into service. Personally, I don't, although I have incorporated them successfully in a number of designs. A kitchen is for cooking. It's only fitting that the tools of the trade be openly displayed—celebrated, if you like.

When there's not a pot or utensil in view, the kitchen becomes sterile, antiseptic. Gone is the feeling that here is where someone actually produces a meal for the family. Gleaming pots and appliances can impart a sense of warmth and well-being to a kitchen, and encourage even more use. Displaying your tools shows your own highly personal work patterns and habits. The mood created is inviting and, yes, even intimate.

Breaking Free of the Kitchen Triangle

A good kitchen, as I've noted, is one that is instantly adaptable to different needs, and can work as efficiently cooking for one as for the maximum number of people you want to entertain. Most homeowners face an immediate obstacle: the kitchen triangle. What is the kitchen triangle? You won't find it in Webster's. You will find it in most American homes, however. For decades, it has been the great bane of sensible kitchen design. The concept first emerged from a 1950s University of Illinois study that attempted to formulate the best use of small residential space for four-person families. Researchers developed an approach to kitchen design that established the three major appliances—refrigerator, sink and cooktop— as the critical three points in the kitchen around which everything else was built.

The refrigerator was placed at one end of the space, the cooktop at the opposite end, and the sink somewhere in the middle (the oven was simply put wherever space allowed). No matter that having these three important stations at distant points in the triangle might create some inconveniences for anyone actually cooking. On paper, it looked neat and tidy and geometric. The triangle concept of kitchen design was quickly picked up by the kitchen design industry. It was an easy way to train young kitchen designers, and it crept into home after home.

There is a basic problem with the triangle, aside from the inconvenient distances. The design is static. With a major appliance located at one of three fixed points, the kitchen physically cannot compress or expand to accommodate greater or lesser amounts of food or numbers of guests. The triangle can't adjust to additional people working in the kitchen at the same time since there are no options for extending the workspace. Yet, as we all know, the kitchen serves an ever-fluctuating number of people every day. The triangle ties the cook's hands. *It is the cook who must adapt to the environment, not the environment to the cook.*

Appliances Drive the Design

Do yourself a favor—get the notion of the kitchen triangle out of your mind entirely. Instead, think in terms of flow. Good flow is the ability to cook for 2, 4 or 10 without having to walk more than a few steps in any direction, no matter how large your kitchen is. Most kitchens are designed for a minimum number of people, not the maximum, and that's the mistake. *Always design for the maximum not the minimum.* But, with proper flow patterns, you can actually double your workspace without breaking down a wall.

Think also in terms of the tools you need to cook. The options today are so much greater than they were in the 1950s, thanks to the virtual revolution in appliances. A range was once the sole hot cooking spot in the kitchen. Today, we speak in terms of cooktops and ovens, toaster ovens, microwaves, convection ovens and combination microwave/convection ovens—and those aren't even the exotic options now available, such as built-in grills, deep fryers and woks.

Is it any surprise that when I'm asked what the most important element of kitchen design is, I answer, "Appliances, appliances, and more appliances"? Few people realize that poor appliances can render a magnificent kitchen nonfunctional when cooking for more than four. So, a point I cannot stress enough: *The limitations of your equipment determine the menu for the life of your kitchen.*

When you are designing your kitchen, keep in mind not only what appliances you need, but how they will be used. A microwave oven, for example, should be placed next to the refrigerator, since most of what you cook in a microwave comes directly from the refrigerator or freezer. Adding a second sink (one for prep work, the other for clean-up) becomes a must, to both break the triangle and give the space versatility. The two-sink design, when spaced properly, splits the workload and allows for separate flow patterns.

This splitting of functions is liberating if you can see the possibilities. They will allow you to break free of the kitchen triangle, and to create new spatial relationships. (See illustrations A through D.)

To show you more exactly what I mean, let's say you are about to cook a dinner for eight. Your menu consists of a lettuce, tomato and mushroom salad with balsamic-cilantro vinaigrette dressing; pan-fried chicken piccata; zucchini with roasted peppers and walnuts; and new potatoes with roasted garlic, onions and fresh rosemary in olive oil.

You start preparing the red potatoes first since they take the longest to cook. You have to wash the potatoes, peel and wash the garlic and onions, and wash the rosemary. You have now used the sink three times.

Next comes the salad, which really ties up your sink. You wash maybe two kinds of lettuce and then the tomatoes. If you don't have a second sink, no one else can help and you clearly can't prepare the chicken or the zucchini until you have finished these tasks.

Now you are making the dressing for the salad, and you need to use the food processor or blender or at the very least a jar to combine the cilantro, olive oil, vinegar and other seasonings. In the meantime, you have roasted your potatoes, your garlic and onions, so now you have those pans to contend with. And you haven't even gotten to the zucchini, which will take another pan; the roasted peppers and walnuts, which will require yet another oven tray; or the chicken, which will require one or two frying pans.

In short order, it is clear that the sink will be sky-high with oven pans, frying pans, a salad spinner, a strainer and the various utensils you've used.

The big question now is: What do you do with the dinner dishes? Wouldn't a second sink be nice? You might say that this menu is too much work. Yet not one of these dishes is difficult unto themselves. With a second, well-placed sink—regardless of whether or not you are the type of cook who cleans up as you go along—this menu would be a snap.

If you're thinking that your kitchen is simply too small to accommodate a second sink, take a look at the illustrations at the end of this chapter. They prove that you can break the kitchen triangle in virtually any size kitchen.

This is just one example of ideas I'll deal with more thoroughly in later chapters. The basic point, for now, is this: Most of us deliberately simplify our menus because our kitchens don't allow us any options. The ability to sauté, steam and grill at the same time is (we think) impossible, so typically we limit ourselves to the most ubiquitous of menus: a salad made in the sink, a roast with baked potatoes in the oven, a vegetable cooked on top of the stove, a dessert either bought or made in advance. Anything more interesting or complex demands so much extra labor due to the inadequacies of our kitchen layouts and our appliances that we don't usually attempt it. If we do, we start cooking Saturday's dinner on Wednesday. The true joy of making such a meal is thus diminished, or missing altogether.

The Subsystem Approach

As rational human beings, we derive great pleasure from creating order out of chaos. We try to break down a process to a series of steps. We try to develop a system.

Think of the kitchen as just such a system, one demanding order, but flexible enough to be versatile. Think of cooking as a process that must be broken down step by step. Each step corresponds to, and makes use of, a part of the kitchen system. Each of those parts are subsystems of the overall kitchen design. If you can imagine designing your kitchen with an understanding of the cooking process and the subsystems involved, you will not only have gained valuable insight into cooking itself, but will very likely end up with a kitchen that responds beautifully to your cooking needs.

Sound a bit confusing? Let's run through the stages of cooking a meal to demonstrate what I mean. Pretend it's that moment when you walk into your kitchen to plan a meal for 12. You begin thinking about your guests, their tastes, the time of year, whether it's brunch, lunch or dinner, how elaborate an effort you want to make. Planning is part of the whole process.

The first subsystem is where you plan the meal: a kitchen desk area, with bookshelves to house all your cookbooks, notepads and pens, perhaps a log book of past successful menus, a telephone.

Then, once you've shopped, you need adequate unloading and storage space, both dry and cold—other subsystems. Planning, storage, food preparation, cooking, clean-up—all of these are subsystems. If any one of them is missing or not functional, the process breaks down. The result for you is harder work, longer time in the kitchen, potential chaos and a lot less enjoyment.

In the following chapters, we'll take a look at each of these subsystems, how to make efficient use of them, and how to avoid common design pitfalls.

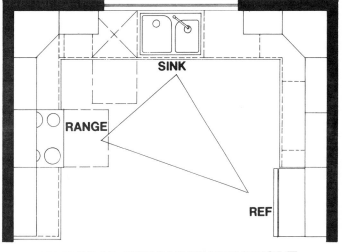

TYPICAL KITCHEN TRIANGLE

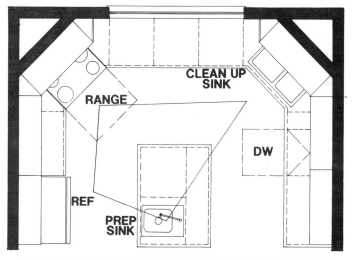

BREAKING THE KITCHEN TRIANGLE

ILLUSTRATION A

12

RANGE

REF

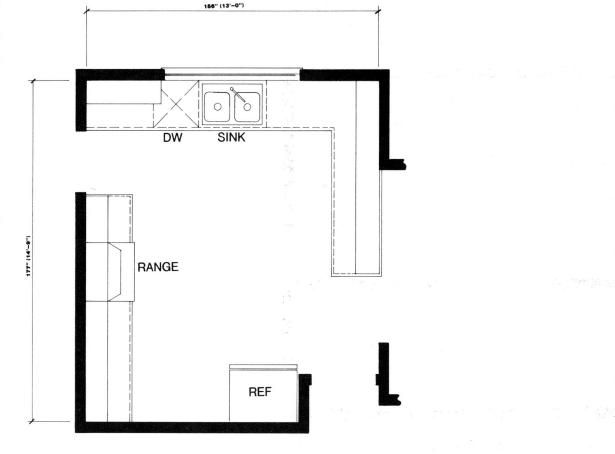

156" (13'-0")

177" (14'-9")

DW SINK

RANGE

REF

BEFORE

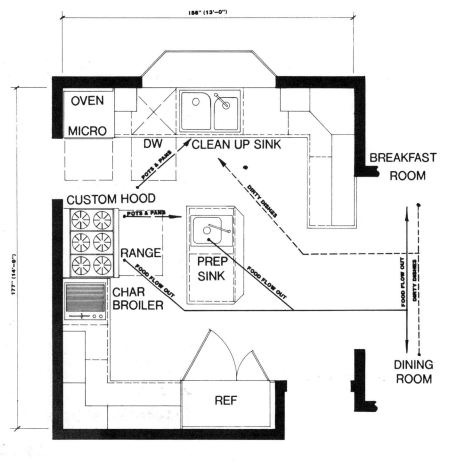

156" (13'-0")

OVEN

MICRO

DW CLEAN UP SINK

POTS & PANS

CUSTOM HOOD

POTS & PANS

RANGE

FOOD FLOW OUT

CHAR BROILER

PREP SINK

FOOD FLOW OUT

DIRTY DISHES

BREAKFAST ROOM

FOOD FLOW OUT

DIRTY DISHES

DINING ROOM

REF

177" (14'-9")

ILLUSTRATION C

AFTER

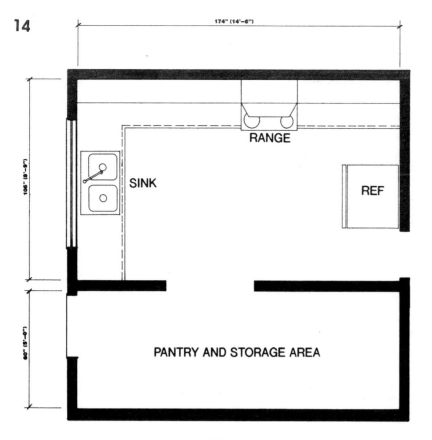

174" (14'-6")

106" (8'-8")

60" (5'-0")

SINK

RANGE

REF

PANTRY AND STORAGE AREA

BEFORE

ILLUSTRATION D

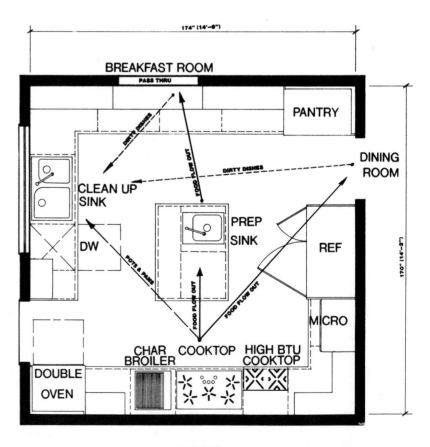

174" (14'-6")

170" (14'-2")

BREAKFAST ROOM

PASS THRU

PANTRY

DIRTY DISHES

FOOD FLOW OUT

DIRTY DISHES

DINING ROOM

CLEAN UP SINK

PREP SINK

REF

DW

POTS & PANS

FOOD FLOW OUT

FOOD FLOW OUT

MICRO

CHAR BROILER

COOKTOP

HIGH BTU COOKTOP

DOUBLE OVEN

AFTER

Notes

Notes

Chapter 2

STORAGE SUBSYSTEMS

The first element in good kitchen design is the storage subsystem. By storage, I mean both dry storage, or cabinetry, which holds everything from plates, pots, pans, utensils and dry and non-refrigerated foodstuffs; and cold storage, or the refrigerator/freezer, which maintains the perishables.

Cabinetry Dry Storage

When you walk into a kitchen, your first impression likely comes from its cabinetry. It's usually the most dominant feature and tends to set the tone aesthetically. Cabinetry can also dominate a kitchen design budget: It generally represents between 25 and 50 percent of a kitchen's total cost.

As important as it is, both in terms of style and function, cabinetry often presents a formidable obstacle to good kitchen design. In a proper kitchen, it is the appliances that drive the design, and the cabinets work to support appliance placement. But the cabinet industry has long set the standards when it comes to dimensions. In a sort of tail-wagging-the-dog situation, manufacturers create appliances to fit into the cabinet industry's standardized 22-in.-deep European to 24-in.-deep American cabinets. Stop for a moment and consider the consequences: Cooktops are designed to fit a cabinet, not to address whether you cook for 2, 6, 12 or 20 people.

This problem can often be addressed by having your cabinetry custom built, a pricey but worthwhile expense. While you'd have a hard time customizing a stove, oven or sink, you can, and should, get exactly what you want, and need, in your cabinetry.

Where do you begin? A local cabinet shop? A home improvement center? A furniture store? A kitchen showroom? A contractor? An architect or designer? The process can make your head spin. I find that, for most of my clients, the best way to begin is to decide which period or style you like—country, Shaker, contemporary, and so on. You will begin to get a picture in your mind of what your kitchen will look like. Then, sit down and figure out realistically how much storage you need. Then decide how much money you can spend.

But be generous with your estimate—remember that your cabinets are the resting place for everything in your kitchen. If you choose poorly, or shortchange yourself, you won't be able to extract those cabinets without ripping out the countertop, disconnecting the appliances, and almost certainly ruining both your floor and walls. In later years, your kitchen cabinets, if properly designed and constructed, will outlive you. Now is your chance to do it right.

But what is right?

☐ Your options

Roll-out shelves, spice drawers, pull-out pantries, pantries of varying depths, vegetable drawers, built-in lazy Susans, wine racks, tilt-out wastebaskets, built-in cutlery dividers, tray partitions, lid storage racks, tray and cookie sheet storage racks, door racks for packaged foods—these are just some of the options today's innovative cabinetry designs offer. (See illustration E.) And they can make your life infinitely easier. Take the usual pot-and-pan storage cabinet. You oftentimes end up on your hands and knees to find that one pan you need sitting at the very back of the cupboard. A simple roll-out shelf pulls straight out of the cabinet to fully expose everything on it.

There are basically four types of cabinetry on the market today: stock modular, semi-custom modular, custom modular and custom millwork. Let's look at them one at a time, from the least to the most expensive.

Stock modular. You've seen it at your local lumberyard, home improvement center or kitchen warehouse. Stock cabinetry, which is premanufactured and sold right off the floor, is most frequently used by builders, contractors and do-it-yourselfers. As the least expensive option available, stock cabinetry offers few options. You may be able to choose between two door styles, one to three finishes, and limited sizes and configurations.

Most 24-in.- or 30-in.-wide wall and base cabinets of this type have a center stile, or post, running vertically through the center of the cabinet's interior for structural support. Stiles are inconvenient in that you must reach around them to retrieve items. Another drawback to stock cabinetry is that you will end up designing your kitchen around the cabinets, rather than having the cabinets conform to your needs. Unless you're really pressed for dollars, I wouldn't consider this option.

Semi-custom modular. If money is a problem and anything custom is out of reach, I would consider semi-custom modular cabinetry an acceptable option. These lines are a cut above plain stock cabinetry in that they offer a greater variety of sizes and styles. Rather than one or two door choices, you may have a dozen to choose from. The selection of stains and laminates with different finishes is more diverse. Unlike stock cabinetry, which can be purchased straight off the shelf, semi-custom modular cabinetry must be ordered. But don't deceive yourself: You still must essentially design your kitchen around these cabinets.

Custom modular. Most companies offer custom modular cabinets in 3-in. increments, up to 36 inches in frameless and 48 inches in framed. However, you can customize these cabinets to measure any size. You can also order angled or rounded (known in the trade as radiused) cabinets. Some brands of custom modular cabinets can be ordered elaborately carved, or hand-distressed for an aged look. Some lines are very high quality—a fact reflected in the moderate-to-high price tag. But well worth it.

ILLUSTRATION E

SPICE DRAWER INSERT

KNIFE DRAWER INSERT

PULL OUT CHOPPING BLOCK

PULL OUT IRONING BOARD

TILT DOWN DRAWER FRONT

PULL OUT TOWEL BAR

STAINLESS STEEL BREAD BOX

MIXER LIFT

VEGETABLE BINS

PULL OUT TABLE

PULL OUT COUNTER

PULL OUT PANTRY BASE

CAN STORAGE DOOR RACK

PULL OUT TRASH CAN

DOUBLE PULL OUT TRASH CAN

Custom millwork A good local cabinetmaker can create a kitchen to your exact needs and specifications. There are many positives to ordering custom millwork. For one, the craftsman is right there in front of you, able to make adjustments or correct mistakes as you request.

The major advantage, of course, is that custom millwork (as well as custom modular) cabinetry serves, and does not dictate, the overall kitchen design. The big negative is that a local cabinetmaker will not be able to give your cabinets any finish that is as good as the catalytic conversion-varnish finish (more about this later) that custom modular cabinets feature.

☐ Choosing cabinetry

Most people don't realize that the cost of cabinetry generally relates to how the door is made, what the door style is, and what type of wood or laminate is used. Twenty feet of cabinetry may cost $10,000 if the door is plain. But, give the door a simple raised panel and the price jumps to between $12,000 and $14,000. A raised panel door requiring multiple moldings and a good deal of manual labor may run $20,000. Add angles or rounded edges and you could be looking at $25,000 to $30,000. If you want the door in a formed polyester, you're at $60,000.

Although there are many cabinet door styles, there are only two kinds of cabinet "boxes": framed and frameless. A framed cabinet features a vertical member, or stile, and a horizontal member, or rail. The hinges attach to the stile, and the box comes with either an inset door, which sits flush with the frame, or an overlay door, which sits on top of the frame. A frameless cabinet has no stiles or rails. It is simply a box with hinges placed inside. (See illustration F.)

There are differences between the two that go beyond how they look. For example, if you want a frameless angled, double-access or sink cabinet, it will have to be strengthened. Frameless cabinets can also cost you more because of their size. You can specify a 48-in. framed cabinet, but you generally don't want to go beyond a 36-in. frameless cabinet because it is not structurally sound. So if you choose frameless cabinets, you may need more of them.

American base cabinets run 34-1/2 inches high. The toe kick is 4 inches high by 3 inches deep. European cabinet manufacturers make their toe kicks 6 to 9 inches high, in order to line up with the standard 36-in.-high American counter and American appliances. You need to know these differences in sizes, because if you choose European cabinetry you will lose 2 to 5 inches of cabinet storage space, and in a small kitchen inches count. (See illustration G.)

Of course, there are many cabinet manufacturers, and a wide range of cabinets to choose from. Given the same kitchen design, you can find yourself with bids anywhere from $10,000 to $80,000. The difference in price reflects the materials used, the intricacy of the craftsmanship, the quality of the hinges, whether the drawers pull out completely or only

CABINET CONSTRUCTION

FRAMELESS   FRAMED

TALL CABINET

WALL CABINET

BASE CABINET

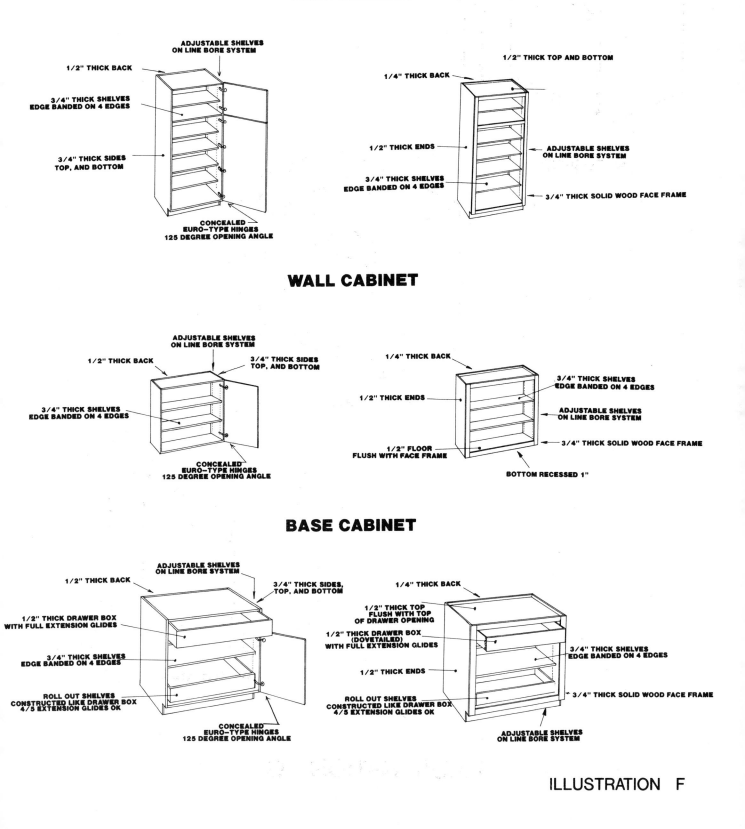

ILLUSTRATION F

DIFFERENT HEIGHT TOEKICKS

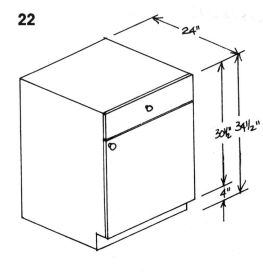

4" TOEKICK

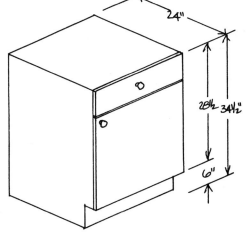

6" TOEKICK

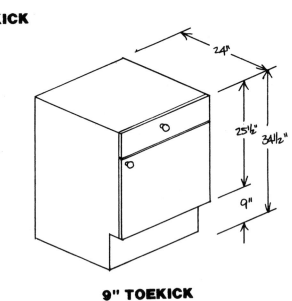

9" TOEKICK

ILLUSTRATION   G

three-quarters of the way, the amount of customizing you desire, and the uniqueness of the style. Whatever you choose, be sure you have the measuring and   installation done by whomever you've bought the cabinets from rather than your own carpenter or contractor. That way, if there are any problems, they won't become yours.

Materials and finishes. Most cabinets are made of oak, maple, pine or birch. Other, more exotic and rare woods such as cherry and walnut will cost you more. Particleboard, which ranges from low-grade sawdust to high-grade compressed wood slivers, is often covered with a laminate, or resin-soaked sheets of paper pressed together to form a veneer. The thicker the laminate, the stronger and more durable the cabinet will be.

Given a cabinet of decent quality, the finish determines its durability. Wood furniture can take any number of finishes—paint, colored lacquer, polyurethane, oil, varnish. Kitchen cabinetry, however, because of its exposure to moisture, grease and grime, stands up best with a baked-on catalytic-conversion varnish. Nothing on the market today holds up as well. Not only does this finish make your cabinet impervious to kitchen wear and tear, it is nearly maintenance-free. The one problem with this finish is that it is generally only available on modular cabinetry, and usually beyond the facilities of your local custom cabinetmaker. A good way to test whether your cabinets can stand the test of time is to dab a hidden spot with some acetate or nail polish remover. If the finish stands up to it, the cabinet is likely to be impervious to household chemicals and cleansers, marking pens, food stains and most other common kitchen threats as well.

Refrigeration Cold Storage

Cold food storage is, essentially, no different than dry food storage. Refrigerator manufacturers like to have you think in terms of cubic feet. Resist. Think instead in terms of shelf space. By doing so, you'll be much better able to assess your needs and find the appliance that addresses those needs.

When you shop for a refrigerator, you will have a choice of side-by-side (refrigerator on right side, freezer on left), over-under (freezer on top, refrigerator below) and under-over (freezer below, refrigerator above), in sizes that include 24 inches, 30 inches, 36 inches, 42 inches and 48 inches. (See illustration H.)

Most people use a refrigerator far more than they do a freezer. The general rule is that a person goes to the refrigerator between 17 and 21 times more often than they do to the freezer. The over-under is therefore the least useful model—you must bend constantly to retrieve anything. Even though it is the most energy-efficient model on the market (it may save you $20 a year on your electric bill), think about the human energy it wastes. However, if the choice is between a 36-in. side-by-side or an over-under with a 36-in. freezer on the bottom, take the over-under. The alleged convenience and larger capacity of a 36-in. side-by-side is wasted since the freezer takes up disproportionate space for its frequency of use. Vital refrigerator space has been sacrificed, and the result is a refrigerator incapable of

DIFFERENT REFRIGERATORS

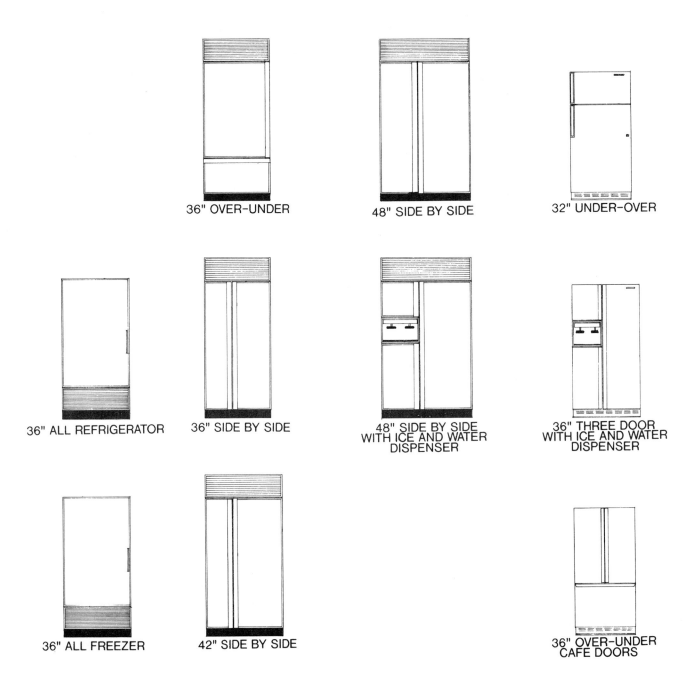

36" OVER-UNDER

48" SIDE BY SIDE

32" UNDER-OVER

36" ALL REFRIGERATOR

36" SIDE BY SIDE

48" SIDE BY SIDE
WITH ICE AND WATER
DISPENSER

36" THREE DOOR
WITH ICE AND WATER
DISPENSER

36" ALL FREEZER

42" SIDE BY SIDE

36" OVER-UNDER
CAFE DOORS

ILLUSTRATION H

accommodating a number of bowls or platters of food prepared ahead of time for a party.

Single-door refrigerators can be hinged to open either right or left, depending on your space. Refrigerator doors on side-by-sides, whether the 36-in., 42-in. or 48-in. model, hinge only on the right. Thus, in designing with a side-by-side in mind, both the sink and the countertop must be to the left or you will constantly have to walk around your refrigerator door to put anything down. Picture yourself reaching into such a refrigerator and pulling out a quart of milk in one hand, a plate of butter in the other. How do you shut the door? Your choices are your foot or your backside. It bears repeating: Placing the sink and countertop to the left of a side-by-side is essential.

Single-door models are generally 24 to 36 inches wide, and between 60 and 73 inches high. There are new built-ins, however, that run 36 to 48 inches wide and 84 inches high. One manufacturer offers a model with a roll-out freezer on the bottom and a pull-out step to reach a wine cooler on the top. Its refrigerator section has equal-size double doors that open from the center. While the overall space is the same as in a standard refrigerator, each door is narrower than standard and thus requires less space to open out. This model works well in a small kitchen, or in a tight area created by a center island.

With the advent of under-counter refrigeration, any combination of 24-in.-wide refrigerator and/or 24-in.-wide freezer units can be specified. Refrigeration options can multiply by installing more units where they add to convenience. The small size of these units allows them to fit into unusual or simply small places.

Some people like the look of commercial refrigerators. These models come in a variety of sizes, all in stainless steel, some with stainless steel doors and others with glass doors. Glass doors, while attractive, don't offer many benefits. For instance, you can't have shelves on the door. Certain models also have a depth of only 24 inches, though some make up for the loss of space in height—84 inches versus the standard 64 to 67 inches. These shallower units do have the advantage of lining up with the standard base cabinets so the refrigerator doesn't jut out into the room. And gone are the days when you would find a container at the very back of a shelf containing a green substance that was once tomato sauce. With 24-in.-deep refrigerators, all food items are at your fingertips.

A final note on refrigeration: Ideal internal temperature should range between 36 and 40 degrees Fahrenheit. Most manufacturers achieve zone temperatures and humidity control through drawers and other closures for butter, cold cuts, vegetables and fruits. Tomatoes will thrive best in the butter area, where the temperature is around 50 to 60 degrees. Fish and shellfish will do best in the back of the refrigerator, where the temperature is a few degrees colder because it is less effected by the opening and closing of the door. If you have any concerns about your refrigerator's temperature setting, by all means buy two or three temperature gauges so you can test its different dial settings.

Notes

Chapter 3

FOOD PREPARATION SUBSYSTEMS

Good prep space means that everything you need is within two or three steps. This includes your food processor and other small appliances, your cooktop, oven, pots and pans, and prep sink. But the single most important element of a good food preparation system is lots and lots of counter space.

Counters

One of the biggest problems most clients articulate to me concerns kitchen counter space: There simply isn't enough of it, or it's in the wrong place. They are right. As far as I'm concerned, most kitchens do not have enough counter space, and it is in the wrong place. Several culprits are to blame. The kitchen triangle is one. The sink, stove and refrigerator positions dictated where the counters ended up, not where counter space was actually needed. A more basic problem can be traced back to the building practices of the '20s and '30s and, more specifically, to the ubiquitous 4-ft.-by-8-ft. plywood sheet. Back then, it was customary to set studs 16 inches apart. It was also customary to create 8-ft. ceiling heights. The 4-ft.-by-8-ft. plywood panel conveniently spanned floor to ceiling and three studs. That piece of plywood also determined the size of the wall and base cabinets. A contractor could simply order the panels in bulk, using some for walls, then slice the remainder down to create counters and cabinets. And so, in most older houses, base cabinets measure 22 inches deep and wall cabinets 12 inches, creating a 22-in.-deep counter.

None of this did much to promote efficient function in the kitchen. It was all a matter of convenience and economics for the builder. Base cabinet depths were later modified to 24 inches to accommodate the advent of the built-in dishwasher. To my mind, however, the 24-in.-deep counter still isn't deep enough for most kitchen work. Not only is there no space to lay things out, but it becomes impractical to leave out the small appliances you need to have handy for food preparation. If you do keep them out on the counter, you've got no room to work. You're forced to labor vertically rather than horizontally.

What do I mean by "vertically" and "horizontally"? It's natural, and optimally efficient, for us to spread out our work so that everything is easy to see and easy to reach. When we don't have enough horizontal, or side-to-side, space, we start to work vertically—we stack, in other words. Containers are placed on top of containers, utensils and packages are placed on top of refrigerators or ranges or in sinks, or anywhere we can find space. Does this sound painfully familiar? There is salvation, however. It comes in the form of the 30-in.-deep counter.

☐ The 30-in.-Deep Counter

When I began to consider what a cook truly needs to prepare food properly, I thought, how nice it would be to take cold food from the refrigerator, a roast from the oven, the vegetables from the range, all at the same time—and still have space for the small appliances that have been employed to make these dishes. All this can be accomplished with a 30-in.-deep counter. How do you get such a marvel? There's no real mystery. You simply set the traditional 24-in.-deep base cabinets six inches away from the wall and extend the counter back to the wall. This process is called "furring out" the cabinets. To answer the question I know you're about to ask, yes, you can see a 6-in. space from the side. That's not a problem—just be sure to order a 30-in.-deep side panel and the space will never show.

If you have any doubt what a wonderful work surface the 30-in.-deep counter creates, (see illustration I). Notice how much counter space there is, even with the small appliances sitting at the back of the countertop. With such a design, your food preparation surface is working for you, not against you.

☐ Counter surfaces

There are five basic counter surfaces. I'll go over them in order of least to most expensive.

Post-formed and custom laminates. Decorative laminates are created much like puff pastry, layer upon layer. The process uses different kinds of papers, soaked in resin, then pressed together using about 1,200 pounds of pressure at a temperature of 280 degrees Fahrenheit. Laminate makes an excellent surface, both aesthetically and functionally. It resists scuffs and stains, and its smooth surface is easy to clean and maintain. Post-formed, or prefabricated, laminates and custom laminates are made the same way. The difference between the two are design options and price, with custom running about double the price per square foot as the post-formed. The relatively inexpensive price tag of laminates is their main attraction, as well as the fact they have no grout lines to collect dirt and stains. On the other hand, should you scorch, burn or cut a laminate surface, you'll need to replace the whole piece.

Ceramic kitchen tile. Kitchen tile, a traditional and reliable choice, offers you an extraordinary range of options in terms of colors, patterns and sizes—everything from 4 inches by 4 inches to 12 inches by 12 inches. I prefer to use a minimum of 6-in.-by-6-in. tiles because they minimize the number of grout lines while offering a range of design options. Tile will take hot pots and can be combined successfully with other interesting materials, such as granite or solid surfaces. You do end up with the dread grout lines, although in a contemporary pattern, the grout line can be a butt joint as thin as 1/16 of an inch. In a rustic, country-style design, however, the tiles should feature a large grout line of 3/16 inch or 1/4 inch—clearly a case of form over function.

It is easy to be dazzled by the variety. But there are important questions to ask. Will this tile hold up on a kitchen counter? High-gloss tile, for example, does not stand the test

30" DEEP COUNTERS

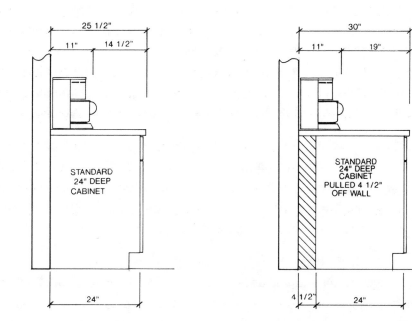

PLAN USING 30" DEEP COUNTERS

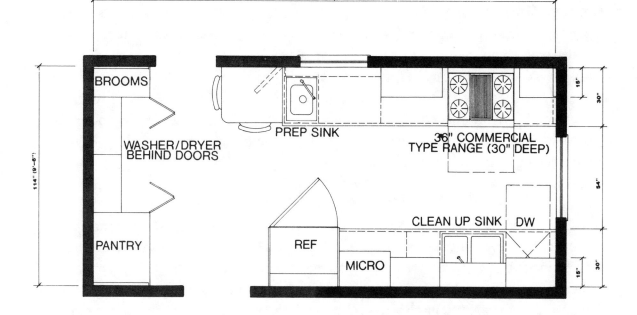

ILLUSTRATION I

of time because the finish will dull and scratches will show. A better choice is a matte finish. Another question: Are trim pieces available in this pattern? The edge of your counter requires a curved piece of trim called a bullnose or V-cap, the counter corner needs inside or outside corner pieces, the sinks also need corner pieces.

You may want to mix tiles to your personal taste, but this can be problematic since tiles vary in length and width as well as depth. If you do want to mix them, I strongly advise you to hire the best tilesetter you can find or you may end up with an expensive disaster.

Wood. Wood is certainly a beautiful material. And if the counter is built from hard maple butcher block, it will provide a smooth, durable surface you can use a knife on. There are real problems with wood, though. It requires heavy maintenance—it should be bathed in mineral oil every three months to prevent it from drying out and cracking. It can also scorch, burn and stain easily. And, wood carries a moderate to expensive price tag.

Solid surfaces. Solid surfaces generally are composed of resins, polyesters and/or acrylics. The mix depends on the manufacturer, who usually trademarks the name. Regardless of which product you choose, solid surfaces are wonderful because they take abuse better than any other counter surface. Solid surfaces are nonporous and resist staining and burning. Also, since the color runs equally through the entire piece, you can repair minor burn marks and scratches by rubbing it with steel wool or 320-to-400-grit sandpaper. On the down side, solid surfaces cannot take a hot pot, color choices are still limited, and it is expensive.

Granite. With its range of color textures, granite is one of the most exciting, and dominating, materials in kitchen design today. Its surface is like glass, it cleans easily, is hard to stain if sealed properly and will take a hot pan. Granite is, however, one of the most expensive surfaces you can use. It also can overpower your kitchen design aesthetically.

After reading this list, I'll bet you want to know which one I recommend. I'll sidestep that answer by saying your choice should depend on your personal taste and on your budget. All of these surfaces will, in fact, function quite well, especially with the addition of trivets and cutting boards for the more delicate ones.

Small Appliances

Whether your kitchen is tiny or spacious, tools and equipment that you use daily should be literally at your fingertips to save you time and energy. The problem comes when you have a kitchen with limited counter space and you must keep the countertop clear of appliance clutter in order to work. If you have adequate depth, however, and can store your appliances at the back of the counter, make sure your backsplash, or the covering between the top of the counter and the bottom of the wall cabinets, is at least 15 to 18 inches high. If you have sufficient cabinet storage—and you're tall enough—I would recommend the 18-in. height. This means the bottom shelf of the cabinet will be four feet, seven inches from the floor.

Consolidating small appliances can go a long way toward maximizing what counter space you do have—and by consolidating I don't mean gathering them all together in one spot; I'm talking about consolidating functions. For example, a mixer, blender and standard food processor can all be replaced by one of the new breed of food processors, which can cut, chop, blend, whip, knead, slice, strain, shred, julienne, puree—in essence, do everything those other appliances can do together. The many accessories for these new processors can be neatly housed in a drawer, and the processor itself can be stored on a pull-out shelf that swings up and locks into place at, or just below, counter height. Food processors can handle about 90 percent of all prep work, although cooks who do a lot of baking may feel they need a heavy-duty mixer as well.

Another space-saving option is appliances that attach to the underside of wall cabinets, effectively lifting them off the counter entirely. These include can openers, coffee makers and knife sharpeners, which come in cordless and plug-in varieties.

Built-in food centers are motors set directly into the counter that attach to a food processor, blender or other appliance. They are worth considering for small kitchens with minimal counter space. These machines can mix, blend, grind coffee, crush ice and perform a dozen tasks in a compact space. While food centers are helpful in a small kitchen, they are actually a liability in a large kitchen, since they are stationary and thus limit work flow. For large kitchens, I recommend appliances that can be moved from here to there.

The new kid on the block is the immersion blender. It looks like a stick with blades at one end and a handle at the other, attached to a long cord and plug. This strange beast is called a blender, but it actually is a blender/hand mixer hybrid. Not only can the two-speed immersion blender accomplish everything the blender can, it can also whip cream and beat egg whites into peaks. The cord makes it portable, so you can, if you choose, puree a sauce right in the cookpot. It is small and easy to clean, and can hang from a bracket fastened to the counter backsplash to relieve counter clutter. As far as I'm concerned, the immersion blender is one of the most efficient pieces of equipment to hit the marketplace in a long time. My two pieces of advice for its use: Employ tall pots because it can spatter, and always start on low speed, then move to high for thorough mixing.

Chapter X includes an appliance-frequency survey designed to help you figure out your cooking patterns and needs. Use it!

The Prep Sink and Other Prep Areas

The counter is the main, but not the only, preparation area to consider when designing or redesigning your kitchen. A little creativity, combined with common sense, can gain you both extra space and efficiency.

Take, for example, the notion I spoke about earlier—the second sink. I will talk about the specifications of sinks more fully in Chapter VI, the clean-up subsystem, but I can't pass up another opportunity to lobby for the addition of a second sink in the kitchen. This second sink, as I've mentioned, I think of largely as the cook's sink, to use for food preparation, while the first sink functions almost solely for clean-up chores, or as a second prep area when you are preparing for a large party. A second sink is just the type of utility station that can break the kitchen triangle, split the workload and create separate flow patterns for the different tasks each handles. As such, it is well worth the cost. But make sure dirty dishes can travel directly from the table to the clean-up area without crossing the path of the prep area. Also, if the distance between the prep sink and the clean-up sink is too great, you may want to consider a dishwasher for the prep area as well.

For a preparation sink, I recommend a single, deep bowl. It should be a minimum 16 inches wide, although I myself prefer 24 inches because I clean my pots and pans as I go. A good prep sink must be deep enough to handle your biggest pots and whatever rinsing, soaking and washing tasks are at hand. The prep sink should be either tile-in, which means flush with the counter tile, or under-mounted, in which case the sink sits below the counter surface, so that food scraps can be easily swept from counter to basin.

This is not the only helpful food prep option. Another one I like a great deal is the rolling table. A kitchen needs to be a minimum 12 feet wide to accommodate a 24-in.-deep island, which even at that only allows for a 3-ft.-wide aisleway. So if you don't have a 12-to-14-ft.-wide kitchen, you can still very effectively extend your counter space by using what is actually a type of rolling island. The rolling table can be used as a stationary unit, and fitted with an overhead rack to hold pots and pans. If it has a drawer and a lower shelf, you end up with additional storage space. (See illustration J.)

But the rolling table's best feature is its mobility. It can roll from the refrigerator to the sink or the range as needed for actual cooking or food preparation. When covered with a tablecloth, it turns into a movable buffet that can be rolled straight into the dining room for service. Then, it can roll right back into the kitchen with the dirty dishes for clean-up.

The rolling table offers the type of flexibility that makes a kitchen an effective workplace, since it allows you the freedom to redefine your work space as you need it. Rolling tables come in a variety of surface-area sizes, from 18-in.-by-18-in., up to 2 1/2-ft.-by-5-ft. Any size larger may present mobility problems. In other words, you need to make sure it can pass through the doorway between your kitchen and dining room.

Other prep area helpers include an inset stone slab for pastry rolling. Make it granite, not marble, since marble is very porous and can stain and spot easily. All counter materials, with the exception of butcher block, dull knives, so it is critical you cut on a wood cutting board. Set it next to the sink, so scraps can be easily swept away. Make sure you reserve a wide drawer in the prep area for your utensils, and a cupboard for your bowls and measuring cups. All of these ideas will speed along your prep process and cut down the energy you need to get the job done.

ROLLING TABLE

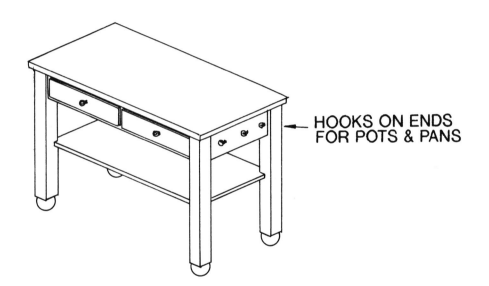

HOOKS ON ENDS
FOR POTS & PANS

ILLUSTRATION J

Notes

COOKING SUBSYSTEMS

As I've mentioned, inadequate counter space forces a cook to work vertically rather than horizontally. A poorly designed cooktop will victimize you in the same way. If your burners are small and close together, you must use smaller, taller pots, which then require you to constantly stir the contents so the food at the bottom doesn't burn and the food at the top isn't undercooked. Think about it: How many recipes have your read requiring top-of-stove cooking that you realized you couldn't prepare because your burners were inadequate?

Cooktops

Generally speaking, the four factors to consider when buying a cooktop are the number of burners, the distance between the burners, the adequacy of the heat and the efficiency. Having said this, I must add that almost none of the standard American or European cooktops work particularly well. As a whole, they are poorly designed. The burners are not large enough, they do not emit enough heat, and they are badly placed in relationship to one another. (See illustration K.)

Cooktop manufacturers have not kept pace with today's cooks. Take sautéing, which requires large front burners that give off high heat. You would think manufacturers would place them where they belong. Unfortunately, that's not the case. Most cooktops have one small and one large burner in front; others have two small burners in front and the larger burners in back.

These configurations made some sense at one time, when a small front burner was needed to melt butter or do other tasks requiring a small pan and a low flame. But today, microwave ovens take care of those kinds of jobs faster and better. What we now need from our cooktops are larger burners with better control—burners that can handle a 13-in. pan when cooking for large groups, and quickly switch from high heat for sautéing to low heat for poaching.

One of the most important considerations for any cook purchasing a cooktop is the strange term "recovery ratio." Recovery ratio, in the commercial kitchen world, means the amount of time it takes for the fat or liquid in a pan to get back to the temperature it reached before adding the food to be cooked. Think of making pasta. You bring the water to a rapid boil, then add the pasta. The recovery ratio is the amount of time it takes for the water to again come to a boil. The lag time matters less for boiling pasta than it does for, say, pan frying, when you start by heating some type of oil or butter and then add the poultry, fish or meat. Immediately, the oil or fat loses much of its heat. The slower the recovery ratio of your

DIFFERENT STANDARD COOKTOPS

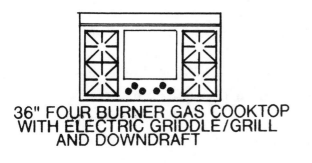

36" FOUR BURNER GAS COOKTOP
WITH ELECTRIC GRIDDLE/GRILL
AND DOWNDRAFT

36" FIVE BURNER GAS COOKTOP

36" FIVE BURNER GAS COOKTOP
WITH DOWNDRAFT

36" ELECTRIC COIL COOKTOP
WITH GRIDDLE/GRILL
AND DOWNDRAFT

36" FOUR BURNER
ELECTRIC HOB COOKTOP

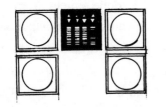

MAGNETIC INDUCTION COOKTOP
(SHOWN TWO DIFFERENT WAYS)

30" GAS COOKTOP

ILLUSTRATION K

cooktop, the greasier your food will turn out.

Recovery ratio is linked to the amount of heat, or British Thermal Units (simply, BTUs), a gas burner generates. One BTU equals the amount of heat required to raise the temperature of one pound of water one degree Fahrenheit. In an electrically powered cooktop, energy is measured not in BTUs but in watts. Watts translate to BTUs on the order of roughly one to four: 1,000 watts equals about 4,000 BTUs. An electric cooktop's large burner, or element, generates 1,800 to 1,900 watts, which equals 7,200 to 7,600 BTUs; while small elements run 600 to 800 watts, or 2,400 to 3,200 BTUs—technically. I say technically because, in reality, gas cooktops lose 25 to 35 percent of their heat (unless the burner is sealed) so an electric cooktop's large element is roughly equivalent to something more like a 12,000-BTU gas burner.

☐ Your options

I'm often asked what type of cooktop I recommend. You have basically four choices: gas, electric, magnetic induction and halogen. Gas is the most popular by far, so I'll start there.

Gas. Professional cooks use gas more than any other source of heat. Of course, they're playing in the big leagues: A burner on a professional cooktop generates between 15,000 and 25,000 BTUs; the average residential gas burner produces between 6,000 and 10,000 BTUs. This disparity can make a significant difference in the quality of the food you're sautéing.

Have you ever asked a restaurant chef to give you the recipe for a certain dish you love, then tried it at home and it just didn't work? He insists he gave you the right recipe; you insist he must have left out a secret ingredient. What the two of you do not realize is that the key ingredient is heat!

Still and all, gas provides the home cook with the greatest number of options. You can see the size of your flame, and you can control it instantly.

Gas cooktops feature combinations of one, two, four, five, six or eight burners, and run from 36 to 48 inches wide and 24 inches deep. As I've mentioned, you want to know the amount of BTUs the burners generate, the size of the grate that the pot or pan sits on, and the distance between the burners. You also want to know how large a pan will fit on each burner. Shopping for a cooktop, then, becomes much easier if you take along your largest frying pan or stockpot.

A 13-in. pan will fit nicely on some cooktops that have been on the market for three or four years. They feature four to eight burners and are 24 inches deep with 11-in.-square grates. One company, by special order only however, offers a 27-in.-deep cooktop with 12-in.-square grates. All of these cooktops generate between 15,000 and 20,000 BTUs per burner. These, to me, are the most desirable cooktops available. Many clients assume they don't need a cooktop this big, this powerful and that looks this commercial. But looks can be deceiving. These are the only cooktops that give you all your options.

I have a couple of cautions about cooktops with sealed and heavy-duty burners that generate 12,000 BTUs and up. Simmering can be difficult without the use of a heat diffuser, or metal plate that sits between the pan and the burner grate to lower the amount of heat transferred. Luckily, heat diffusers are inexpensive and can be found at most hardware or kitchen supply stores.

Also, be wary of any continuous grate, oftentimes referred to as an "S" or "V" grate because of the design. Even after you have turned off the heat, the temperature will remain constant for a considerable length of time, so you need to make sure you slide the pot or pan to another area of the cooktop. This type of grate can also be dangerous to your hand, so take care!

Electric. Most electric cooktops, which generate about the same energy as gas cooktops, have all the same inherent problems: not enough heat, small element size, not enough distance between elements. Still, some clients prefer them. They claim electric is cleaner and produces no gas fumes, which is certainly true. Electric cooktops come with two, four, five or six elements. I recommend six, since the response time for heating and cooling electric elements is notoriously slow—in fact, the wait can drive you crazy. My advice for electric cooktop users who know they will need both high and low heat while cooking: Pre-heat two elements, one high, one low, then simply move your pan when you need to.

Electric cooktops offer a choice of element styles: coil, hob or flat top. Coil, a metal heating element in a spiral shape, allows you to see if the heat is on or off, since the coil turns red when hot. The slightly raised hob is opaque and usually black, which looks neat and clean, but you can't see whether the heat is on or off; also, large pots and pans tend to trap the heat and cause the element to turn off. Flat tops, made from ceramic glass, are the worst, in my view. You can't see the heat and spillage is a real cleaning problem.

Magnetic induction. The only types of pots or pans you can use on a magnetic-induction cooktop are those made of ferrous metal, that is, cast iron, steel or triple stainless steel. Unlike traditional cooktops, magnetic-induction surfaces do not have a direct heat source, such as a flame or coil. Magnetic induction works by causing the pan's metal molecules to vibrate, thus creating energy, which generates heat. The four-burner cooktop itself stays cool, although after a pan is removed you can feel the heat left by the pan's bottom.

Magnetic induction, while absolutely superb for low-heat tasks such as melting chocolate or butter, steaming and poaching, cannot generate enough heat for sautéing. Given sufficient time, a cast-iron skillet will be able to reach a sufficient temperature, but it will also stay very hot for a long time since cast iron dissipates heat relatively slowly. Thus, you lose control over your cooking process.

One company produces magnetic-induction cooktops with four separately controlled 12-in.-square ceramic tiles in a variety of colors. I have used this system many times in my designs, and while it is not inexpensive, it creates a wonderful look and the tiles function as countertop when not in use. I like to place the tiles in a single row for ease of use or, if there is room, to checkerboard them with regular ceramic tiles in-between.

For efficiency, I add two gas burners with 13,000 or more BTU capacity, side by side if space allows. The average cook rarely needs more than two high-heat burners. This combination of gas and magnetic induction gives you the best of both worlds—high heat when needed, and efficient low heat that is easily accessible. If ever a magnetic-induction cooktop with 3,000-watt elements comes on the market, buy it!

Halogen. This cooktop makes use of halogen gas, which is contained in a tube that sits under a glass surface. Halogen works on the same principle as an incandescent lightbulb. However, the name is somewhat misleading: On a halogen cooktop, only one or two burners actually use halogen gas; the others are electric.

The halogen element is not quite equivalent to a large electric coil in the amount of time it takes to heat up, but the amount of heat it can generate is about the same. Also, halogen cooktops require darker-colored pans, because light-toned pans reflect the heat back to the core of the tube, which results in uneven cooking. Like electric elements, halogen also takes a significant amount of time to cool down.

To me, the major difference between halogen and electric cooktops is the cost of purchase and the cost of repair—halogen will run you about four times that of electric. When all is said and done, it's strictly bells and whistles. As a colleague of mine put it: "The halogen cooktop is good for people who want to heat canned soup and scramble eggs. It's not for the serious cook."

Other Cooking Surfaces and Equipment

☐ Your options

There are a few other choices—and necessities—you need to consider before your cooking decisions are complete.

Charbroilers. With today's emphasis on low-fat cooking, charbroilers are a terrific addition to any kitchen. These units generally consist of an iron grill over simulated charcoal briquettes, with a catch pan underneath. Not only are meat and fish wonderfully tasty, but vegetables turn out extraordinary.

Although you can choose between gas and electric charbroilers (see illustration L), the smart choice is gas for one critical reason: It offers an additional thousand degrees of heat. The flavor in grilling comes from melting fat, which hits the coals, turns to smoke, then rises and adheres to the food's surface. The greater the heat, the more smoke it creates, and the tastier the food.

There is only one gas charbroiler on the market. It comes in both 19-in. and 29-in. depths. However, there are a number of electric charbroilers to choose from. They range in size from 12 to 24 inches wide, are about 22 inches deep, and sit comfortably next to the cooktop.

For years, I had a love/hate relationship with my gas charbroiler. I loved cooking on it but hated cleaning it. I was tempted to throw it into my self-cleaning oven, but the manu-

CHAR BROILERS

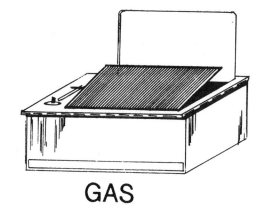

GAS

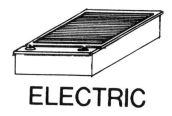

ELECTRIC

ILLUSTRATION   L

facturer's instructions said not to, lest the porcelain finish burn off the grate. Porcelain, aside from its general attractiveness, helps to prevent foods from sticking.

Then one day a client of mine told me not to worry about the porcelain finish. He told me to simply brush my charbroiler with an oil that has a high burning point (such as corn oil) before using it and the food would never stick. Then the grate can be placed in a self-cleaning oven. Suddenly, clean-up becomes a breeze.

Griddles. A few manufacturers now show griddles with their cooktops and ranges. At first glance, it seems like a good idea. The positives are the ease with which you can cook up pancakes, crepes, bacon and sausages. However, you lose two burners in order to accommodate it. Griddles also do not allow immediate adjustment of heat. They are high maintenance—requiring frequent oiling to prevent rust—and may be dangerous when there are children around since there is no visible heat source. From my point of view, the negatives far outweigh the positives. Instead, buy a griddle that fits on top of the range or cooktop burners, or an electric griddle that sits on the counter.

Hoods/ventilation systems. The kitchen's ventilation system is often an afterthought for many clients. In fact, ventilation is critical to the proper and healthy functioning of any kitchen. Ventilation systems should be considered as important a purchase as any other major appliance.

There are a variety of ventilating systems on the market today, including ceiling and wall fans (which are basically worthless), recirculating units (which merely move air around in the hood and back out into the room) and downdraft and updraft systems. The only ventilating system that really works is an updraft unit, which requires a hood. Equipped with a blower, the system pulls smoke through a filter, then out through a duct cut into the roof or the side of the house.

Hood and ventilation systems are rated in cubic feet per minute of air movement, or CFMs. Since vapors rise, you want to make sure you have a large enough container, or plenum, to catch them all. Rather than delve into these more technical aspects, let me simply describe to you what you need.

The hood should extend three inches beyond each side of your cooktop or range, six inches on each side if you also have a charbroiler. For example, if your cooktop or range is 36 inches wide, your hood should be 42 inches wide. The depth of the hood should be at least the depth of your range or cooktop. I prefer three inches beyond manufacturers' recommendations.

Height from the floor is unimportant, since the hood has sufficient CFMs to draw all the waste. Many times I have put the bottom of the hood 72 to 76 inches off the finished floor, rather than the standard 57 to 66 inches, so that taller people can walk under the hood without banging their heads. In order to place it that high, however, you need to double your CFM capacity for a normal cooktop, which generates a total 30,000 to 40,000 BTUs, or 300 to 400 CFMs. If you add a charbroiler, you will need a second CFM motor, a second duct

DOWNDRAFTS

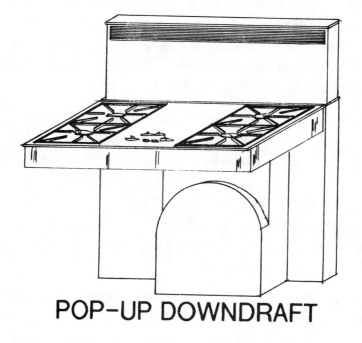

POP-UP DOWNDRAFT

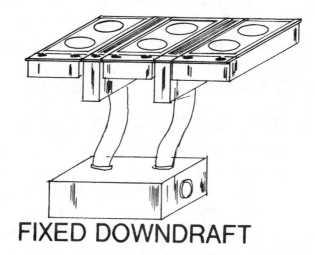

FIXED DOWNDRAFT

ILLUSTRATION   M

and separate switches—a variable speed switch for the cooktop area, and a fixed speed switch for the charbroiler area.

I've often had people ask me why the hood doesn't pull the smoke out completely. I've suggested opening a window and, lo and behold, it works. In commercial kitchen design, we worry not only about pulling out pollutants, but about pulling in good air. In a residential kitchen, opening a window usually will do the trick.

On occasion, I've had to use downdraft ventilation systems, which pull the smoke down and out a floor duct under the house. This can be necessary when the cooktop is on an island and you don't want to use a hood because it appears too massive or if structurally you can't vent up.

In these situations, cooktops generally take one of two kinds of ventilation systems. One lies flat, centered between the burners. The other rises six to seven inches behind the cooktop. (See illustration M.) Of the two, there is no question that the latter is superior. It is elevated over the cooktop, giving it a better chance to catch pollutants. Both, however, are imperfect because they cannot capture all the rising vapors the way a plenum can.

Ovens

There has been a virtual revolution in oven design since the days of the single-range oven. No longer relegated to "wherever space could be found," today's ovens can perform an array of tasks, and have become integral in good kitchen design.

☐ Your options

Five types of ovens are available on the market today: the standard electric radiant oven, the convection oven (the true convection, and the fan-assisted), the microwave oven and the convection/microwave oven.

Electric radiant. This oven is the one most familiar to us. It has two heating elements, one positioned at the top for broiling, the other at the bottom for baking and roasting. In some of the newer units, both top and bottom elements can be used for baking. In the standard radiant oven, heat rises from the bottom of the oven to the top, pushing the cold air down but also creating hot and cold spots that can result in uneven cooking. We all know what it's like to put two trays of cookies on an oven's two shelves. The cookies on the bottom cook much faster than those on the top because they are closer to the bottom heating element, and the trays must be reversed halfway through the baking time or the cookies on the bottom end up burnt and the cookies on the top end up undercooked. For my money, there is a better oven on the market: the convection oven.

Convection. There are actually two types of convection ovens available today: the true convection, and the fan-assisted. Most domestic ovens are fan-assisted, which simply means that the manufacturer has added a fan to the back of the standard electric radiant

OVEN HEATING SYSTEMS

RADIANT OVEN

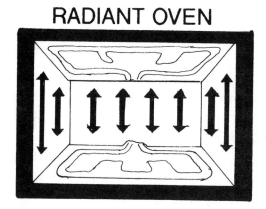

EXPOSED HEATING COILS

TRUE CONVECTION OVEN

HEAT SOURCE

OUTSIDE OF OVEN CAVITY

ILLUSTRATION   N

oven. (See illustration N.) I'm not saying this type of oven isn't good, but it simply can't handle the large volume of food that a true convection oven, with its additional racks, can.

In the fan-assisted oven, the heat comes from the exposed elements at the top and bottom, with the bottom contributing 75 percent of the heat and the top 25 percent. The fan circulates the heat in the oven cavity to eliminate hot and cold spots. This type of oven generally can handle only two racks of food at a time, even though the manufacturer usually provides a third rack. If you use all three racks, you will have to rotate the food at some point, because the top and bottom racks will brown faster than the middle rack due to their direct exposure to the two heating elements.

A true convection oven differs in that the heating element is wrapped around the fan, which causes the heat to flow evenly over all the racks. There are three to four racks in the oven, but you never need to change their positions, even for baking. But that's not the only benefit. In a true convection oven, you can simultaneously place a tray of cookies, a pan of fish and a pan of poultry. The aromas and flavors will not mingle because the continuous air flow prevents odors from escaping.

Convection ovens are beginning to appeal to the consumer for this reason, and because they appear, from the outside at least, to be smaller. That brings me to an important point: the proper way to measure oven capacity. In a standard radiant oven with exposed heating elements, the cooking space is measured from the bottom rack to the top heating element, not from the oven floor to the ceiling. In the true convection oven, there are no exposed heating elements so the entire oven cavity is usable.

Still, as good as it seems, a convection oven is not without its problems. The forced air flow can cause dryness in some foods. Adding a liquid, such as stock, wine or water, to a roasting pan helps combat the problem. But many bakers will not use convection ovens for baking such items as meringues, or anything with phyllo dough or puff pastry, for just this reason.

The beauty of most convection ovens made for home use is that they can switch from convection to radiant, or radiant to convection. You have options, which, as you know by now, is my favorite word. For example, if you have a dining room that seats 10, 12 or 14 people, I would consider a smaller convection oven on top with a larger one on the bottom. Again, don't be deceived by how tiny the small, European built-in convection oven appears. It will easily handle a 20-pound turkey. So you may want two different-size ovens, a small one for daily use and a larger one when entertaining crowds.

Convection ovens are now made 36 inches wide, with the oven cavity 24 inches wide. That means the oven racks, when not in use, are too large to store anywhere in most standard kitchens. Be sure to have your designer specify a base cabinet 12 to 15 inches wide to store these racks vertically.

Microwave. Microwaves are energy sources that cook food from the outside in, by agitating the water molecules in the food, which creates friction, which in turn creates heat. They are, in essence, steam machines. In microwave ovens, the most important quality to look for is wattage—your best bet is to buy the highest possible. The reason is simple: the higher the wattage, the faster the food cooks. You want to be able to cook with low, medium or high heat, in small and distinct time units.

A good microwave cookbook is a must, but be aware that there is no standardization in them. Medium in one book can mean 275 degrees and in another 325 degrees, so you will need to do some experimenting with whichever microwave you choose.

Most of my clients use their microwaves for melting butter, warming leftovers and reheating coffee. Microwaves work in tandem with refrigerators and freezers, and so should always be placed near them. Microwaves can fit on the counter, or be built into a wall cabinet. If you are tight for space and want the microwave off the counter, there are models now that can be hung from the bottom of a wall cabinet.

If you want to fit a microwave into a tall cabinet or into a wall space, be sure to buy a trim kit, or frame that secures the microwave into the cabinet and has a small vent at the top to allow air to flow around the unit. If you want to put an oven into the bottom of a tall cabinet and the microwave up top, leave plenty of space between them since the hot air rising from the oven can damage the microwave's digital pad. One last item to note: All but one manufacturer build microwave ovens that hinge only on the left, so make sure you can open your door the way that makes good sense.

Convection/microwave. I am not referring here to any type of portable countertop unit; I am talking about a full-size, built-in oven, which runs roughly from 12 to 30 inches wide, 12 to 18 inches high, and 15 to 20 inches deep. These ovens have the capacity to cook by microwave or convection heat or both of the above.

These combination ovens can be of great help to the working person who likes to have a home-cooked meal but does not have a lot of time in which to cook it. These ovens allow you, in most cases, to throw in a little microwave power while cooking with convection methods—and they won't change the texture of the food being cooked. While a convection/microwave oven will microwave anything you put into it, don't expect it to replace your 600-to-800-watt countertop unit, which efficiently concentrates the energy in its small cavity. Food takes longer to microwave in a combination oven because the microwave energy diminishes within the larger cavity—you might say it gets "lost in space."

Combination cooking works well with almost any baked good. An apple pie can be baked in half the time and still produce a brown, flaky crust. Most casseroles and stews also do well, but roast meats do not since microwaving essentially steams meat.

A few general closing notes on ovens: All ovens have thermostats. Manufacturers calibrate their ovens very carefully, but with common use and time the calibrations can be off. The best way to check your oven's true temperature, if you have any doubt, is to buy an oven gauge at a kitchen supply store. If there is a discrepancy, and you've had the oven less than a year, most manufacturers will come out and fix it for free.

Also, keep in mind that if you stack ovens, you lose two to two and a half feet of counter space. If you can afford it, fine, but most small kitchens can't. Counter space comes under the heading of high-frequency use, while ovens are low-frequency. Placing both ovens under the counter may mean you'll have to bend a few times a week, but it may be worth the trade-off. It's your decision to make, but ponder it carefully.

Ranges

A range is a cooktop and oven combined in the same unit, designed mainly for space savings. However, the average range measures 30 inches wide, which accounts for the same problems cooktops suffer: The burners are too small and don't generate enough heat.

However, a new type of range is on the market today, incorporating the new breed of cooktops, including griddle and charbroiler options. (See illustration O.) This new range looks commercial, but is specifically made for the home. It is insulated so it can butt up against cabinets without scorching them, and the burners are sparked by electronic ignition. This type of range comes in a number of sizes, from 30 to 60 inches wide. Range depth is 28 to 32 inches, so make sure it doesn't project so far out as to create traffic problems.

The smaller, single-oven range comes in either convection or radiant, and the larger one, with two ovens, comes with one convection and one radiant oven or both radiant. The convection-oven option will add dollars, but to my mind it's well worth it.

A range's big plus is that it saves high-frequency-use counter space. While it may be convenient to have your oven in a tall cabinet, you need to think carefully about how often you use your oven versus how often you use your counters.

Also, if you decide to invest in a range that has gas burners with high BTUs, be aware that it may require a three-quarter-inch gas line instead of the standard half-inch. Don't let it be installed without this adjustment.

NEW BREED 48"
SIX BURNER GAS
RANGE WITH DOUBLE OVENS
WITH GRILL AND HIGH SHELF
BACKSPLASH

NEW BREED 36"
SIX BURNER GAS
RANGE WITH 6" BACKSPLASH

30" FREE STANDING RANGE

30" SLIDE-IN RANGE

ILLUSTRATION   O

Notes

Notes

Chapter 5

CLEANUP SUBSYSTEMS

Washing dishes, glasses, pots, pans. Cleaning produce, fish, fowl, meat. Disposing of containers, wrappings, food waste, peelings. Because this subsystem is so all-encompassing in the cooking process, it deserves as much care and planning as any other aspect of good kitchen design.

Sinks

As I'm sure you've noted by now, I believe strongly in the two-sink kitchen—and I don't mean the traditional two-basin sink. Kitchen clean-up has evolved just as every other kitchen function has. It's time we catch up with reality.

Remember washing dishes as a kid? There was one central sink, made up of two, usually equal-size 13-in. basins. We filled one side of the sink with soapy water to wash and the other side with clear water to rinse. Today, for the most part, we use the sink to simply rinse dishes before we load them into the dishwasher. The dishwasher now performs the function of the first sink, making the 13-in. double-basin sink a dinosaur.

Configuration is the most important factor in choosing a sink. I think the worst sink on the market, as you've probably already guessed, is the standard 33-in. double bowl. The two basins measure a scant 13 inches each, leaving very little room to wash larger pots and pans. However, there are a variety of double-sink configurations, ranging from 33 inches to 48 inches, that work much better even at the 33-in. dimension. (See illustration P.)

Sinks generally come in one of five materials: enameled steel, cast iron, stainless steel, quartz and solid-surface material. I'm always asked which one is the best. My response is, "Which do you like?" If you buy a quality sink, it should last a lifetime regardless of the material.

Aside from solid-surface sinks, which are integral to the countertop itself, sinks are installed in kitchen counters in three ways: self-rimming, or top-mounted; flush-mounted; and under-mounted. (See illustration #P.) A self-rimming sink is the easiest to install, since it simply drops into the hole cut out of the counter. It isn't the best design, though. The rim juts up above the countertop, so when you need to scrape food from the countertop into the sink, you must push those scraps up and over the rim. It's a messy, inefficient and often unsuccessful endeavor. If you must have a self-rimming sink, be sure to buy a cutting board that rises higher than the lip so you can easily slide the scraps for easy disposal.

I prefer either a square, so-called "tile-in" sink, which sits flush with the tile, or the under-mounted, rimless sink. In both of these designs, the sink sits at the same level or lower

DIFFERENT SINK CONFIGURATIONS

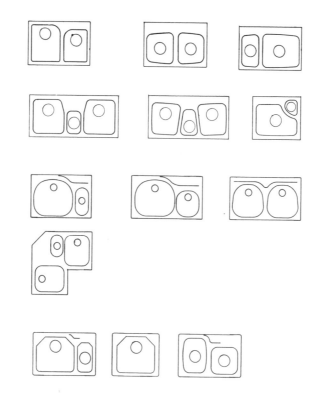

SINK INSTALLATIONS

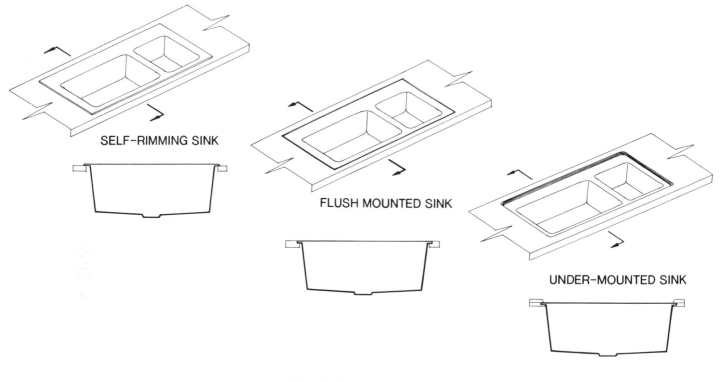

SELF-RIMMING SINK

FLUSH MOUNTED SINK

UNDER-MOUNTED SINK

ILLUSTRATION   P

than the countertop, so wiping food from the counter into the sink for disposal is easy. Single kitchen sinks designed for prep work range from 15 to 24 inches wide. You don't want anything smaller than a 15-in. sink or the garbage disposal will not fit the drain hole. Let your work routine be your guide: If you wash your pots and pans as you go along, then you'll want the largest sink you can fit. If not, you can go with a smaller one. My last piece of advice concerns placement. Almost every home or kitchen design magazine I pick up shows the prep sink in the middle of the island. Don't put it there. A six-ft. island with a one-and-a-half-ft. sink plunked in the middle leaves you a virtually useless two feet and change on either side. Setting the sink at one of the island's ends will gain you four and a half feet of continuous counter space.

☐ Your options

All sinks come with holes drilled into their back ledges, although they can be ordered without them. The holes are to accommodate faucets, air gaps, soap dispensers and other options such as retractable spray faucets for easy clean-up of pots. A standard 33-in. porcelain or stainless steel sink will have four holes. If you need an additional one, be sure to order it. Another note: Strainers and baskets do not come with many sinks, so be sure to order them too.

Faucets. Faucets will require from one to three holes if sink-mounted. There are essentially two types of faucets: single- or dual-control. The single control, which requires one hole, mixes hot and cold water in one valve. The dual, which requires three holes, has separate hot and cold valves. A single-lever type is the most efficient, especially for the prep sink area. When your hands are dirty, or full, you can adroitly maneuver the lever with your elbow. However, single- or dual-control is a personal choice, dependent solely on which you're more comfortable with.

When buying faucets, the price difference has to do with the quality of the metal, valves and surface covering. Some faucets include retractable sprayers, others require a separate attachment. Generally, faucets with pull-out sprayers are more durable, and more expensive.

An air gap, which uses one hole, is required in some states. Air gaps provide a break in the dishwasher drain line, to prevent the drain water from siphoning back into the dishwasher. Check to see if your dishwasher comes with one.

Soap dispensers also require one hole. They consist of an under-counter reservoir and above-counter pump top that allows you to pump soap directly into the clean-up sink. I personally find this option indispensable.

Many people like the idea of an instant hot and cold water faucet, which requires one hole and a switch so you can flip from cold to hot. A small chiller, or refrigerator unit, in the sink cabinet provides you with water cold enough that you don't need ice. A booster, or small hot water tank, heats the water to flow at 190 degrees, hot enough for an instant cup of tea or the best filtered coffee. The one problem with the hot water dispenser: At 190 degrees, it can burn you, so use extra caution.

Water processing systems. There are three popular water processing systems on the market today: filtration, reverse osmosis and distillation. Their main differences are the amounts of minerals they are capable of extracting from your tap water.

Filtration, purchased by about 60 percent of the market, uses carbon and takes out the bad taste but none of the minerals. Reverse osmosis, which is used by approximately 35 percent of the market, passes the water through a carbon and membrane filter, removing about 95 percent or more of all the minerals. Distillation, at about 3 percent of the market, requires a booster heater, which boils water to create a steam that removes 100 percent of the minerals. Your local department of water and power can inform you about these and other systems.

Disposal. Garbage disposals, powered electrically, grind up food. There are two types on the market today: continuous feed, and batch feed.

With continuous feed, you flip on a switch and the disposal starts grinding. You can continually push food waste into the disposal without pausing. The danger is getting your hand caught. Some stores sell a safety unit that sits in the drain and has a flanged top that you push the food through while the water flows to the disposal through veins in the unit's side.

A batch feed is completely safe, since you push down all the food waste first, then insert a stopper into the disposal opening and turn it to start the motor. The negative is that, as the name suggests, you have to grind your waste in batches.

The most important factor when buying a garbage disposal is power. The greater the horsepower, the quieter it will be and the fewer problems you will ultimately encounter. It is better, for example, to purchase a three-quarter-horsepower disposal than a one-half-horsepower unit. There is not much difference in price, and the latter, as it grows older, will more likely break down because it has had to work harder.

Buying a more powerful garbage disposal also makes a difference in warranty. The one-half-horsepower model will generally come with a one-year warranty, while the three-quarter-horsepower carries a five-year warranty.

If you choose a continuous-feed disposal, make sure it features reversible stainless steel blades. These blades will reverse themselves if some material gets stuck, thus maintaining cleanliness and extending the life of the disposal. Spending the extra dollars up front means fewer dollars handed over to the plumber later.

One last piece of advice: If you are tearing up your kitchen, do not even think about re-installing your current disposal. I cannot explain why these units become inoperable when re-installed, but I have consistently experienced this problem over my many years as a designer.

Dishwashers

It's a complete mystery to me why domestic dishwasher manufacturers do not produce residential dishwashers that process faster than the usual 60 to 120 minutes. And, if you're using the pots-and-pans cycle, it can take as long as 140 minutes. That's right—more than two hours. There are, admittedly, several commercial under-the-counter dishwashers that will do the job in four minutes, but these require 240 volts versus the usual 120, they do not dry the dishes, and they are unkind to good china. Domestic American-made residential machines are water guzzlers, consuming 12 to 14 gallons per load.

European dishwashers, on the other hand, are leagues ahead in both speed and water consumption. A few have fast cycles, lasting from 12 to 20 minutes. They will do a good job as long as you do not include pots and pans in the load. Dishes should air dry in a few minutes after opening the door. As far as water use goes, the frugal European machines use a mere four to five and a half gallons, and are quieter.

Most dishwashers today will wash dishes without pre-rinsing. Food particles either collect in a trap, which easily removes for cleaning, or are ground up in an internal disposal system and swept away. As a matter of fact, it is better for your dishes if you don't pre-rinse because dishwasher soap is highly alkaline. Without food residue to work on, the soap works directly on the dish surface, potentially etching it. The soap can also etch glasses and pit silverware. One of the ways you can combat this dishwasher wear-and-tear is to only fill the main soap compartment of the standard two. As it turns out, the water in the first rinse cycle usually isn't hot enough to dissolve the soap anyway.

Almost all dishwashers come a standard 24 inches wide, so your choice of machine will not affect your space planning. But it will make a difference when the time comes to choose your cabinetry, since you may want the dishwasher door panel to match. If the kitchen is very large, or if you throw a lot of dinner parties or have big crowds, you may also want to put in a second dishwasher, in the prep area.

If you are right-handed, the dishwasher belongs to the left of the sink; if you are left-handed, it belongs to the right. All dishwashers come 34 to 34 1/2 inches high, so fitting them under the standard 36-in counter is no problem. However, if you wish to lower the counter, only European models come with adjustable legs that allow the dishwasher to be raised or lowered two to three inches.

The price difference in dishwashers is related to options. The least expensive come with one wash arm, stationary racks and a choice of two cycles. Those in the medium price range offer two wash arms, two to four cycles, a filtering system, a sanitizing cycle that reaches 140 degrees, and some insulation. The most expensive give you three wash arms, adjustable rack positions, adjustable length cycles, a separate silverware rack, a built-in air gap, a hot water booster that raises the temperature by sensor to 140 degrees-plus, and in general far better insulation. Some even feature a built-in water softener, and most are ultra-quiet.

Trash Compactors

Whenever a client requests a trash compactor, I wince. Knowing the many problems that can develop with them, I usually say, "Whoa." For starters, they create odors, and attract insects and sometimes rodents, even when they are kept meticulously clean.

The idea behind trash compactors is well-meaning. Squashing the trash to one-quarter its size saves precious landfill space. But times have changed. Since many cities now require that citizens recycle separate types of trash, trash compactors may have outlived their usefulness. I prefer instead a recycling center located behind a door in a base cabinet next to the clean-up sink. This kind of recycling center is essentially a drawer, which pulls out almost completely on gliders, and has two attached wastebaskets, one for bottles and cans, the other for paper and packaging trash. This system allows for fast and easy separation.

Notes

Notes

Chapter 6

TWO CRITICAL DESIGN ELEMENTS FROM FLOOR TO CEILING

From top to bottom, the design of your kitchen is now complete—almost. While flooring and lighting do not directly fit into any subsystem, they are immensely critical to the proper functioning of each one of them. Now that you have a kitchen that invites you to cook in it, it will do you no good if your flooring isn't easy to clean and, more important, easy on your legs and spine. It also will do you no good if your lighting doesn't allow you to determine when the sauté is just right, much less the ability to read a recipe.

Flooring

Next to cabinetry, your flooring can dominate your kitchen's aesthetics more than anything else. Interestingly, the most expensive choices are not always the kindest on the cook, so you want to think carefully before making a decision.

☐ Your options

There are basically five different kinds of flooring surfaces. I'll discuss them in order of least to most expensive.

Vinyl sheet and custom vinyl. Vinyl sheet goods, manufactured in rolls, are simply cut to the dimensions of your floorspace, then installed as a single piece. Vinyl is easy on the feet and back, and with today's coatings, they clean up to a shine, and do not mark or yellow, unlike yesterday's linoleum. The downside is that if you drop a pot on it, the flooring will dent. Decorative choices are also limited.

Custom vinyl is priced and installed by the square foot, and has the same easy-maintenance and easy-on-the-body features of vinyl sheet. It comes in a wide range of colors and patterns, which can be cut in a variety of ways, then laid in an array of different patterns. Though the seams may show dirt, for the money, there's probably no better choice.

Hardwood. It's beautiful, and because of its "give," it's also easy on the body. However, it is high-maintenance, requiring polishing and immediate clean-up after spills. Pets and children are a terror to it.

Designer woods. Simply stated, designer woods are merely wood flooring that is covered with a clear vinyl veneer. Easy maintenance and kindness to the spine are the positives; the negatives come in its limited choice of grains and colors.

Ceramic tile. Its decorative choices and quality of low-maintenance make it a prime choice for the design-oriented. But it is very hard on the feet and back; items dropped on it will likely break it (and themselves); and any oil and grease spills are a particular danger since they make this surface exceptionally slick. In addition, like ceramic tile on your countertop, you will have to deal with those nasty grout lines.

Natural stone. If you want a kitchen with a rustic look, there is no more enticing choice. But standing for any length of time on a stone surface will make you feel it, and if you drop something on it, it or the item willy very likely break. In addition, you will still have to deal with grout lines, and stone, unlike most other materials, will stain.

Lighting

Complexity is the key word when attempting to recommend lighting choices for the kitchen. With the myriad of different city and state codes, as well as the options offered by incandescent, halogen, fluorescent, recessed, spot and other kinds of lighting, it is almost impossible to tell you how you should light your kitchen. Instead, let me tell tell you where you should light it.

Lamps and fixtures under wall cabinets will light three-quarters of the counter, from the backsplash out. The color of your counter surface will reflect light, so the lighter the counter, the better the light. Your ceiling lamps and fixtures should be placed above the outer quarter of your counter, so that with your cabinet lighting, all surfaces will be lit. Finally, your overhead lighting should cast a balanced light and not leave any dark spots.

Whenever possible, try to use more than one switch for your various lighting. For example, the hood, peninsula, ceiling, under-cabinet and above-cabinet lights in my kitchen all have separate switches, and some are on dimmers. This allows me to light just the parts of the kitchen I'm working in, so it is energy effecient, and it is also a great way to create different moods.

Be sure to have your electrician tell you not only what switches are available but what your various appliances may require. Gone are the days when a small appliance needed only 300 to 400 watts of power. Many today use 700 to 1,000 watts. You need to know if your electrical panel has enough power, and what effect your new appliances may have on your pocketbook.

Finally, wherever there is a counter without water, there should be an electrical outlet, or more if you can accommodate them. Also, have your electrician install the outlets horizontally rather than vertically so your cords don't get tangled together.

In addition, when you're redoing your electrical, your plumbing will be exposed, so now is the time to change all your old pipes. But never remodel without pulling permits from your local city hall. Their inspectors will come to the job site to make sure the work has been done correctly and to existing codes. Then you can feel confident that you are safe and protected.

Notes

Notes

Chapter 7

THE TOOLS OF THE TRADE

A workshop, no matter how thoughtfully or expertly planned and organized, is nothing without the right tools. Pots, pans and knives are the kitchen's basic tools. They work intimately with your preparation and cooking subsystems, yet you'd be surprised at how many clients overlook their importance.

I have had clients spend as much as $250,000 for a new kitchen, yet keep around pots and pans that should have been thrown out years ago. When I design a kitchen, one of my favorite tasks is taking the client shopping for new pots, pans and knives—and helping them understand how purchasing the right tools for their needs can make all the difference.

Pots and Pans

No question, pots and pans are a significant purchase. But choosing the right pots and pans requires the same consideration, and has the same importance, as any other aspect of your new kitchen design.

Most important to understand is that the pot or pan should not control the cook. So the first order of business is to think about the tasks you will undertake with them. Do you need high, low or sloped sides? Is the weight right for the task? For example, if you're steaming vegetables or boiling pasta, you can use inexpensive, lightweight pots. But if you're making stock, you must have a thick, somewhat heavy pot that simmers very gently or your stock will turn dark.

There are other factors to consider: Lids should fit tight. A tight lid is like a tightly closed oven door—it ensures no heat or moisture escapes, and creates a mini-oven on the cooktop.

Another critical element is the pot or pan handle. Does it fit your hand, does it resist heating, can it withstand oven temperatures if need be?

Wood, plastic and assorted metals are the three basic materials for handles. A wood handle will never heat up, and is easy to grip when your hands are wet or greasy. But wood can burn over a high flame, and it cannot go in the oven. Plastic handles have the same heat problems as wood, and also tend to slip in wet or greasy hands. Metal handles often become very hot to the touch, but I use them because they easily go into the oven. But be sure you immediately empty the contents of the pot or pan after use, then place it under water to prevent damage to your counters or danger to your hands. Whatever handle material you choose, make sure it balances with the weight of the pot or pan.

Next on the list of considerations is the size of your cooktop and the spacing of its burners or elements, since they will dictate the size of your pots and pans. For example, if you have 12-in. burners, don't buy a pan larger than 13 inches.

Aside from these factors, the ability to transfer and dissipate heat are the key issues for the cook. How rapidly and evenly does heat transfer to and move through them? How quickly does heat dissipate when the heat source is turned off?

Heat conduction differs according to the type and the thickness of the construction material, and here is where most people go wrong. There is no single "right" material for all your cooking needs. That is the problem with buying pot-and-pan sets—they don't take into account the need for different materials for different cooking tasks.

For example, a slow-cooking stew requires a pot that will absorb heat slowly, steadily and evenly, so that the different flavors can mingle gradually while the meat stays moist. Cast iron fits this bill. Sautéing, on the other hand, demands fast and even heat transfer throughout the pan. But a sauté pan must also dissipate heat quickly—it must cool rapidly the minute it is taken off the heat source because disaster can result if it continues to cook the food at high heat. Aluminum or copper, lined with stainless steel, works best here.

☐ Materials

Let's examine some of the major pot and pan materials, their uses, advantages and drawbacks:

Stainless steel. Stainless steel is one of the most durable materials for cooking, and will not react chemically with foods. Unfortunately, stainless steel diffuses heat unevenly, causing food in different parts of a pan to cook at different rates. Also, it scorches and is difficult to clean. To perform well, stainless steel should be bonded to another metal, preferably aluminum or copper.

Cast iron. Cast iron is excellent for certain cooking tasks. It absorbs heat slowly, distributes it evenly and retains it for a long time. Cast iron works best for cooking stews, casseroles and preparations that go from the top of the range into the oven, such as a pot roast that is braised on the range top, then finished in the oven. However, the very qualities that make cast iron perfect for long, slow cooking make it unworkable for fast cooking processes, such as sautéing. Cast iron also rusts easily, and requires careful cleaning, thorough drying and some maintenance. The unfinished, porous surface of a cast-iron pan must be "seasoned" before the first use, and dried very carefully after it is washed, to prevent rusting. To combat this problem, some cast-iron pots and pans come lined with enamel. The enamel, however, can chip.

Glass. Glass is a hard, smooth surface that does not react chemically with either food acids or alkalis. Although glass can transmit heat quickly and directly, it is a poor choice because it does not transfer heat throughout the pot or pan well. The one cooktop exception is the glass double boiler. It allows the cook to closely monitor the rate at which the water is boiling below, while watching how the food in the upper chamber is doing. Although heat is absorbed only through the glass bottom, and diffusion is poor, in a double boiler this problem is relatively minor. You can accomplish careful and controlled cooking in a glass double boiler, and that is all that matters.

One caution about glass: When you heat a glass pot or pan on the cooktop or in the oven, always add liquid to it. Without any liquid, glass will become overheated and weaken, and likely crack or break on next use. If you forget to add liquid or the liquid has evaporated, you should just throw the pot or pan away.

Aluminum. Aluminum is an excellent heat conductor and diffuser. The metal is lightweight yet tough, and can be used effectively for sauces, omelettes, stews, casseroles and sauté work. However, aluminum's major drawback is that it reacts chemically with acids, and can darken, discolor and change the taste of some acidic foods. A white sauce, for example, may turn gray in an aluminum pot if you've made a tomato sauce in it a week or two earlier. For this reason, some people keep their aluminum pots and pans separated for different uses.

An acceptable alternative is aluminum lined with stainless steel. With these pots and pans, you have aluminum's superlative heat-distribution property combined with stainless steel's non-absorbency. But if you are interested in this combination, make sure the aluminum covers the stainless steel fully because stainless-steel pans made with aluminum only on the bottom do not effectively conduct heat up the sides. One of the best lines on the market is a three-ply bonded design that sandwiches a pure aluminum core between exterior and interior layers of stainless steel. These pots and pans work on any cooktop, including magnetic induction. Most important, even a burnt pan will clean easily and beautifully. They are pricey, but worth it.

Copper. Copper is a wonderful metal for cooktop use. It absorbs heat quickly, diffuses it evenly and dissipates it rapidly. But copper must be lined because it chemically reacts with certain foods and can create toxins. You will generally find copper pots and pans lined with tin, stainless steel or even silver. The quality of the copper can be measured by its feel—the heavier the copper the better.

Copper is also a beautiful sight to present to guests. However, it is very expensive and requires constant maintenance. Its surface must be cleaned with a copper cleaner, or salt and vinegar or lemon juice, to keep it shiny. A silver or tin lining must be watched because it will wear out, and the pot or pan will need to be resilvered or retinned, which is also costly. Sometimes you will find a copper pot lined with aluminum. The combination is wasted, since copper and aluminum both conduct heat well, and aluminum has that absorbency problem. Also stay away from stainless-steel pans that feature a coating of copper on the bottom. You'll pay for the copper, which is too thin to do any good, and you're stuck with stainless steel's drawbacks.

I personally prefer a high-quality copper pan with a stainless-steel lining, because it should never need replacing.

Non-stick. Although non-stick pans are very popular, I don't particularly like them. They change the texture of some foods, and in my book their ease of cleaning is simply not a good enough trade-off. There are any number of non-stick vegetable sprays on the market today, and they even come with garlic butter flavoring and olive oil. If you are diligent about using them, you will never have a clean-up problem. In addition, a good-quality pot or pan requires virtually no more maintenance than a non-stick, and will stand up to much greater abuse.

Pots and pans are complex equipment because you have to think carefully about what you want to cook and how you will cook it. I've summed it up for you in chart 1.

Knives

You cannot cook well without good knives. Period. And notice I use the plural. There's nothing wrong with having one good, all-purpose knife that you feel comfortable using. But one knife will not address all your cooking needs. Specific knives are designed for specific tasks. Take advantage of the many options you can find at a good kitchen or specialty store.

When shopping for knives, you want to buy a forged, rather than a stamped, knife. Forged knives are made from one piece of metal, whereas a stamped knife may be made from several pieces and so is more likely to break. The solid-piece construction of a forged knife makes it stronger. It also has superior weight and balance, which translates into less stress on your hand.

A sure sign of a quality knife is the collar, or the edge of the knife that butts up against your hand on the underside. A good knife will feature a one-half-in.-thick collar, large enough to fit the hand comfortably. The blade should extend into a triple-riveted wood—not plastic—handle, which yields better traction for greasy hands. A quality knife will feel balanced, neither heavier at the tip nor at the handle.

Most knives today are made from a combination of carbon and stainless steel. A full carbon knife will rust if not immediately cleaned and dried after use, but a combination with stainless steel alleviates that problem.

The key to a good knife is sharpness. Whenever you use one, you need to straighten, or steel, the blade edge, called the feather. This is done with an instrument called a steel, or round, which is an elongated steel rod with a rough-grained surface designed to maintain a blade's sharpness. To straighten the feather, you lay the knife on the rod and stroke at an angle with an upward and downward motion. If you are diligent about doing this, your knives will stay sharper longer.

To maintain their effectiveness, knives need to be stored properly. The best all-around knife storage system is a magnetic bar that is designed to maintain the feather. Magnetic bars can be affixed to cabinet sides, to a wall or in a drawer. Placing two bars roughly seven inches apart will enable you to attach an eight-in. or longer knife, such as a chef's knife, bread knife or slicer. The top bar holds the blade, the bottom the handle. Smaller knives will fit completely on one of the bars.

Often, people store their knives in wood knife blocks that sit on the countertop and

Pots and Pans

Material	Heat Dispersion/ Dissipation	Where To Use	Comments	Suggested Use
Stainless Steel	Poor	Stovetop; oven	Needs to be combined with a metal alloy such as aluminum or copper	Water for pasta, soups
Cast iron	Excellent dispersion; poor dissipation	Stovetop; oven	Not good for sautéing; excellent for oven use; requires careful use if lined with enamel, which can chip	Pan frying, braising, stews, pancakes
Glass	Poor	Stovetop; oven	Best use is as a double boiler	Casseroles; microwave
Aluminum	Excellent	Stovetop; oven if lined with stainless steel	Leaches acidic foods if not lined with stainless steel	Boiling, poaching, sautéing, steaming, dark sauces; light sauces if lined with stainless steel
Copper	Excellent	Stovetop; oven	Toxic with most food unless lined with tin, silver or stainless steel; avoid high heat; tarnishes	Boiling, poaching, sautéing, steaming, sauces
Non-stick	Good	Stovetop	Not good for high-heat use since fluorocarbon materials will decompose and emit noxious vapors above 500 degrees F.; can change the texture of some foods	Sautéing without fats

generally hold four to six knives. The advantage is the easy accessibility of the knives. However, every time you pull out a knife from one of these blocks, the edge scrapes the slot's interior and distorts the feather. To avoid this, simply store your knives with the blade up.

Another type of knife storage unit consists of a simple slotted bar with a protective front shield that hangs on a wall or the side of a cabinet. These bars are manufactured in solid surface materials, wood and stainless steel to match different kitchen decors, and can accommodate as many as nine or ten knives. But, as with wood blocks, any time a knife is pulled from its slot it should be steeled.

You can also find, in restaurant supply houses and some gourmet kitchen shops, fabric knife cases with plastic-lined pockets. These cases can hold up to a dozen knives and roll up for easy storage. The negative is that it's difficult getting to a single knife.

Finally, many people, unfortunately, simply toss their knives into a drawer without thought. There is some hope for all of you. A few cabinet companies now make a wooden board, slotted along the top, that fits into a kitchen drawer. Knives can be slipped into the drawer horizontally, so their blades are held firmly in the slots. But again, these knives should be steeled before use. Of course, little of this advice applies to poor-quality knives. You simply can't improve their performance. A good knife, on the other hand, with proper care, will last a lifetime. I am still using the very first knife I bought for the cooking school I attended 32 years ago.

Knives, like pots and pans, are the most basic yet overlooked tools in the kitchen. In chart 2, I give you the basic set I recommend.

Knives

Type	Blade Size	Total Size	Use
French	6 to 8 inches, which-ever is most comfortable in your hand	13 to 19 inches	Slicing, dicing, chopping
Paring	2-1/2 to 4 inches	6 to 10 inches	Slicing and dicing small items
Slicer	8 to 10 inches	15 to 17 inches	Cooked meats
Serrated	8 inches	12 to 13 inches	Bread, tomatoes
Steel	10 to 14 inches	20 inches	Straightening the feather of a blade

Notes

Chapter 8

WORKING WITH A DESIGNER

Finding the right kitchen designer is not simply a matter of finding someone who understands budgets and materials. Sad to say, few in the kitchen design industry ever even talk about the cooking process. Most kitchen designers understand the kitchen from the technical side only. In other words, they may understand all the parts without understanding the whole. But a kitchen is more than the sum of its parts.

If cooking is a priority to you, the key to finding the right kitchen designer is asking the right questions: "Do you cook?" Or, if you are asking for a referral, "Do you know of a kitchen designer who understands the complexity of cooking and baking?"

In other words, can this designer efficiently create, shop for, cook and clean up a somewhat complex meal for eight or more? You want someone who will consider such issues as where the microwave is in relation to the refrigerator, whether you can sauté and bake at the same time, and who understands what poaching and grilling mean and what making a souffle is all about.

I'd be kidding if I said it would be easy to find such a person. Your best sources are through personal referrals, cooking schools and the National Kitchen and Bath Association (NKBA). The NKBA, which encompasses a whole range professionals and companies that manufacture kitchen products, plays a large role in the education of the kitchen designer, including the certification—CKD—that you see after my name on the cover of this book.

To attain the CKD designation of excellence and achievement, a designer must fulfill the following requirements:

• Seven years experience or education in the kitchen industry, with at least two years experience in design planning and installation supervision of residential kitchens;

• Two complete sets of approved drawing documents from actual designed, planned and installed residential kitchen projects;

• Two consumer references pertaining to projects the designer has completed for a consumer;

• Two professional affidavits submitted by allied professionals regarding the designer's competency and work ethics;

• Passage of a day-long, comprehensive examination on the specialized discipline of residential kitchen design, planning and installation supervision; and

• Adherence to the NKBA's code of professional conduct.

Being a proud member of the NKBA, I am certain it can take the one criticism I have of the organization: Its curriculum does not include instruction in the process of cooking or baking. These things must be taught for a kitchen designer to be truly knowledgeable. I am hopeful that classes in these disciplines will soon become mandatory for a CKD designation.

Because of the excellent job the NKBA does perform educating kitchen designers in the construction, technical and cabinetry arenas of the kitchen world, I would only recommend that you interview a CKD, and at least two or three of them. When you find someone you feel comfortable with, ask for the names of three clients who have had jobs completed within the past year. Call those clients and see if they'll let you drop by to see the work.

Then ask them key questions: Did the designer understand the cooking process? Was he or she knowledgeable about appliances? Did the designer stay within budget? Was the design completed within the specified time? Was the designer patient, punctual and in all ways professional? Did you get what you wanted?

When you've chosen your designer, prioritize where you want your dollars to go: space flow, appliances, cabinetry, countertops, flooring. A good designer will be realistic with your budget. If, for example, your budget is $30,000, and the items you've chosen add up to $60,000, a knowledgeable designer should be able to offer you some options. Keep in mind, however, that you will never be able to get a $60,000 job for $30,000. If any designer promises that, run for your life.

The Full-Service Designer

Before you set out to hire a kitchen designer, you need to decide what it is you want done. If, for example, you simply want a facelift—new paint, new countertops, new flooring, new window treatments—you don't need a designer. An interior decorator will do. If, however, you intend to move or replace appliances, reconfigure your kitchen layout or knock through walls, you should consult a kitchen designer. If the work involves knowledge of basic house construction, the kitchen designer may also need to work with an architect or engineer.

The type of designer I am, and the type I am recommending you try to find, is what I like to call a full-service designer. I am unusual in that I am a chef, and care passionately about cooking. My professional obsession is that my clients should be able to use and enjoy their kitchens as much as, or even more than, I do my own. It will come as no surprise, then, that I believe a good kitchen designer should cook with each and every client before putting pencil to paper. I invite my clients into my own kitchen, so they can experience what I consider good space layout and appliances. In turn, I am educated by my clients on the subject of their needs and goals for their new kitchens.

After the first session in my kitchen, I present clients with a questionnaire. It is not only a terrific way for clients to communicate to me what they feel they need, but the questions help us both discover what they want. After going over the questionnaire, I then measure the job site. I take photographs to use as reference, to remind me of what goes on outside in the dining room, the living room, and outside the windows and doors.

The next step is typically going appliance shopping. By this point you know that I believe the appliances should drive the design. I simply cannot understand what to do with a kitchen space until I know which appliances are going into that space. I have found that a good-looking design that simply leaves holes to fill in the appliances may look spectacular but probably won't cook well.

With the appliance information in hand, I am then able to do rough plans, which enables the client to see on paper where everything goes. This I call our "conversation plan." I explain what I've done and why. The client can then say, "I like it," "I don't like it," or, in most cases, "I like this, but can we move that?" The basic floor plan is worked out to both our satisfaction, and at that point, we go cabinet shopping.

Now we are looking at pure style, and the client is fully in charge. All I'm looking for is what type of door style the client chooses, whether the cabinets are framed or frameless, and whether the chosen cabinet line poses any design limitations for such elements as angles or a curved radius.

Once the cabinets are chosen, I draw up a proper floor plan and open elevations, or a straight-on view of the cabinets—without doors drawn—in order to show the shelving configurations inside the cabinets. These open elevations present a second conversation opportunity. The client and I sit and discuss what goes into each and every cabinet: drawers, roll-out shelves, silverware holder, location of trays and so on. Once this task is accomplished, we go shopping for the right countertop surface. Then for flooring, then window treatments.

I am now ready to assemble a complete set of plans, which will include a floor plan and elevations created to the specifications of the cabinets the client has chosen. The plans also include perspective drawings so that the client can clearly see how the kitchen will look; plus mechanical, electrical, lighting and, finally, demolition plans. (See the complete set of plans at the end of this chapter.)

With the kitchen plans package complete, now comes the time to bring in contractor bids. This job generally falls to the client, although I will in all cases help interview if it is desired. Once the client has chosen the contractor, the project is underway. I remain available throughout the construction phase should a problem or other need arise.

When the kitchen is finished, I usually take my client shopping for pots, pans, knives and any other appliances they may lack or need to replace. The final service I provide is to cook a meal for 8 to 12 guests with the client. This gives me the chance to help them adapt to the new kitchen, teach them about their new appliances and perhaps even give them a more efficient way to cook.

There, in a nutshell, is my process. On average, it requires 75 to 100 hours for the simpler jobs, and for more complex projects, between 175 and 250 hours. Every designer works differently. The key is that you convey your needs and wishes. Do not feel shy about being assertive, offering suggestions and insisting on joint decision-making. Educating yourself is the only way you can become partners with your kitchen designer...and end up with a kitchen design with cooking in mind.

How a Design Fee Is Calculated

Designers have two things to offer—time and creativity. There are those who will not charge you a design fee, but they will make their honest profit through marking up the cost of the cabinetry, counters and other materials you buy. To my mind, the selling of product has nothing to do with design—and can get in the way.

If a designer's profit comes from selling you certain products, it will undoubtedly limit creativity. This is why I have chosen to work the way I do, and why I recommend you work with a designer on an agreed-upon hourly rate or a flat rate for the whole job. A significant amount of time goes into accomplishing a good kitchen design. Here is a breakdown of my process:

1. Consultation—Determining what the client wants, needs and how much they can spend: 5-15 hours.

2. Cooking with the client in my kitchen—Talking with the client about kitchen design in the context of cooking: 4-6 hours.

3. Shopping for appliances—Making the client aware of what's available in the marketplace: 4-6 hours.

4. Creating and presenting the rough flow plan—Showing the client where the appliances go and what the traffic patterns will be: 15-50 hours.

5. Shopping for cabinetry—Taking the client to various showrooms that carry cabinetry within the budget: 5-15 hours.

6. Layout, open elevations and perspectives—Illustrating for the client on paper just how the kitchen will look: 10-20 hours.

7. Plan review—Planning with the client what goes into every drawer and cabinet, what special cabinetry is needed: 2-6 hours.

8. Shopping for countertops and flooring—5-15 hours.

9. Reviewing lighting, electrical and mechanical: 5-10 hours.

10. Interviewing contractors—2-6 hours.

11. Following through on job completion—20-60 hours.

12. Shopping for small wares—3-5 hours. 13. Cooking dinner in the client's new kitchen—6-8 hours.

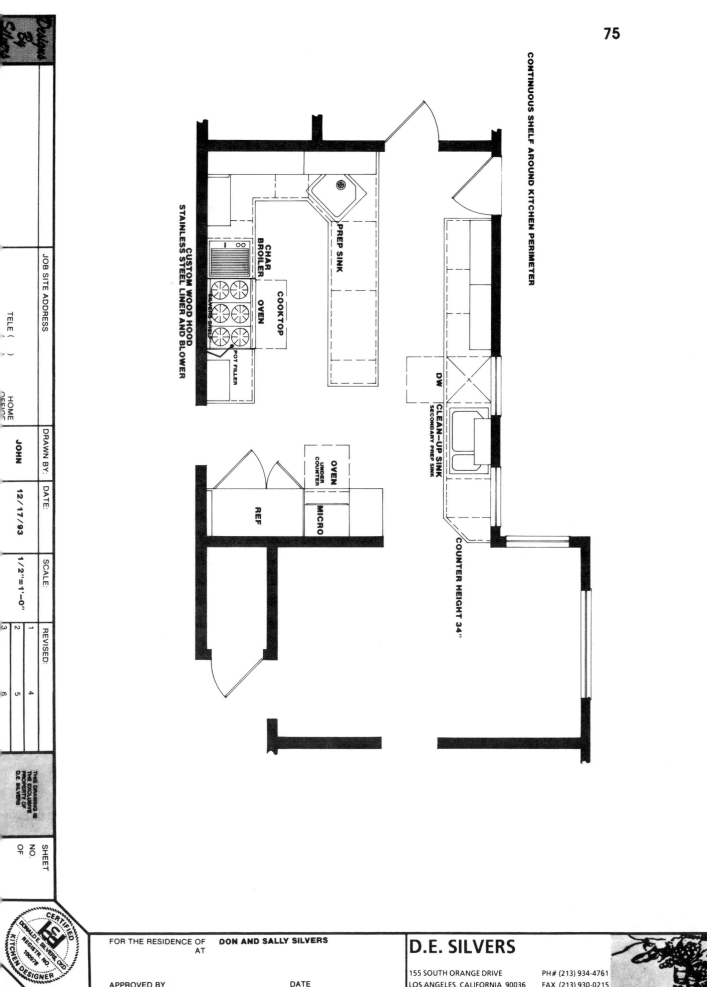

CONTINUOUS SHELF AROUND KITCHEN PERIMETER

CUSTOM WOOD HOOD
STAINLESS STEEL LINER AND BLOWER

PREP SINK

CHAR BROILER

COOKTOP

OVEN

POT FILLER

DW

CLEAN-UP SINK
SECONDARY PREP SINK

COUNTER HEIGHT 34"

REF

UNDER COUNTER
OVEN

MICRO

JOB SITE ADDRESS

TELE ( )

HOME

DRAWN BY: JOHN

DATE: 12/17/93

SCALE: 1/2"=1'-0"

REVISED: 1 2 3 4 5 6

SHEET
NO.
OF

FOR THE RESIDENCE OF **DON AND SALLY SILVERS**
AT

APPROVED BY   DATE

D.E. SILVERS

155 SOUTH ORANGE DRIVE   PH# (213) 934-4761
LOS ANGELES, CALIFORNIA 90036   FAX (213) 930-0215

CERTIFIED
DONALD E. SILVERS CKD
REGISTR. NO. 10078
KITCHEN DESIGNER

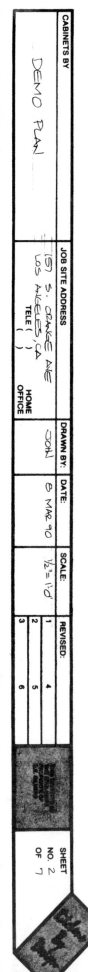

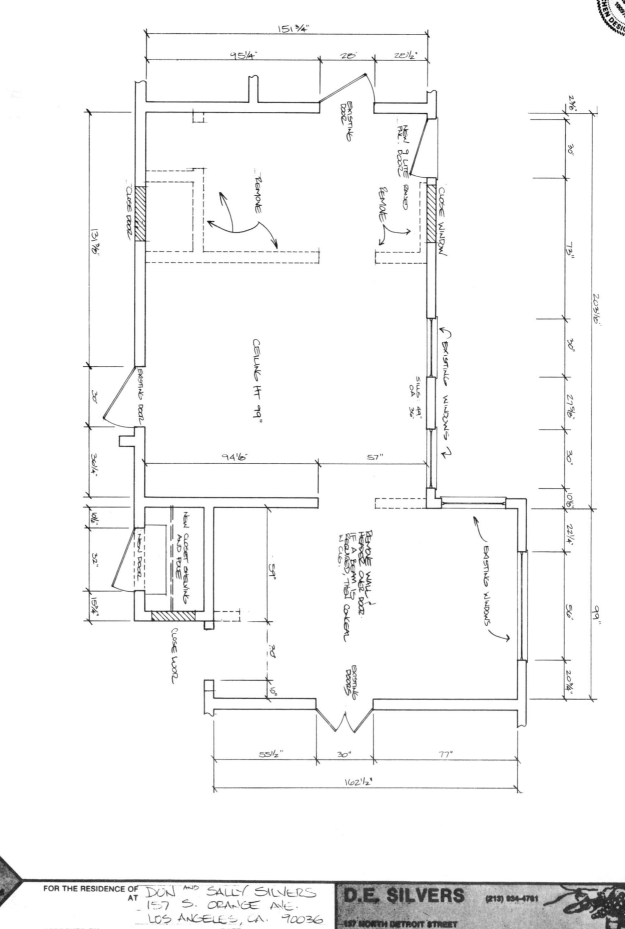

JOB SITE ADDRESS

155 S. ORANGE DR.
LOS ANGELES, CA 90036
TELE ( )

HOME
OFFICE

DRAWN BY: JOHN

DATE: 6 FEB 90

SCALE: N.T.S.

REVISED: 1 4/12/90 | 2 | 3 | 4 | 5 | 6

THIS DRAWING IS THE EXCLUSIVE PROPERTY OF D.E. SILVERS

SHEET NO. 3 OF 7

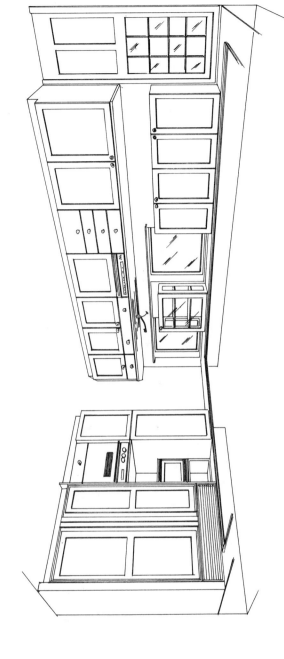

FOR THE RESIDENCE OF DON AND SALLY SILVERS
AT 155 S. ORANGE DR
LOS ANGELES, CA 90036

APPROVED BY ___ DATE ___

D.E. SILVERS
155 SOUTH ORANGE DRIVE
LOS ANGELES, CALIFORNIA 90036
PH# (213) 934-4761
FAX (213) 930-0215

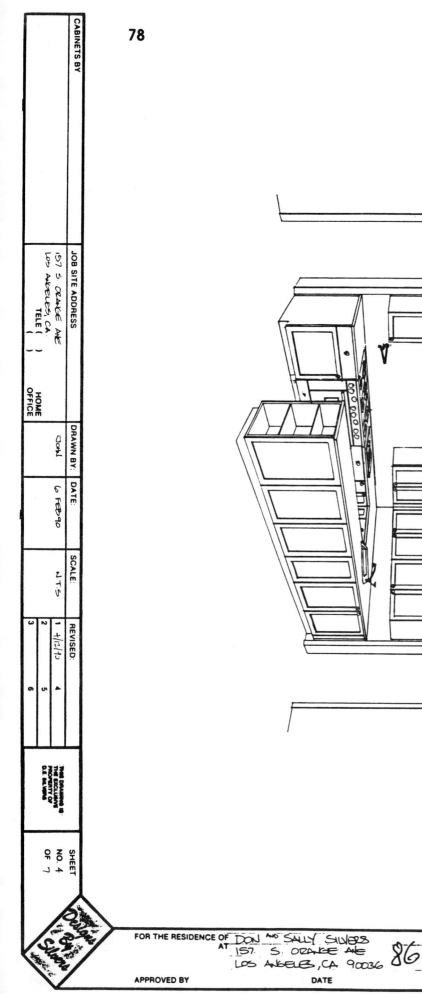

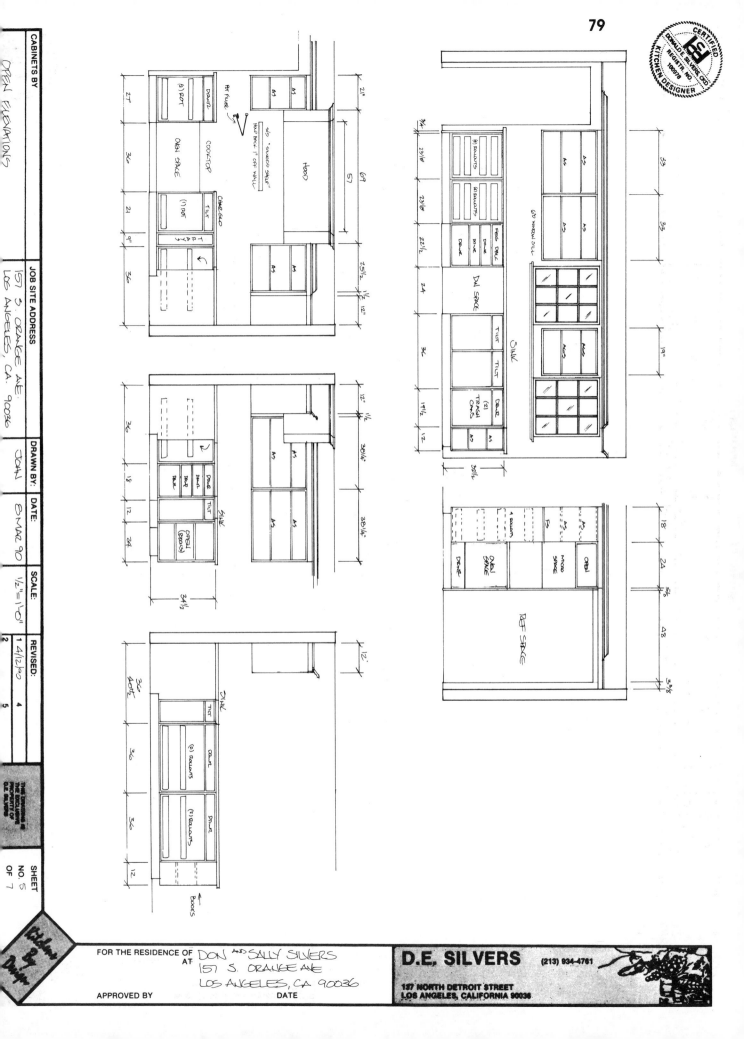

CERTIFIED KITCHEN DESIGNER
DONALD E. SILVERS CKD
REGISTR. NO. 10897

CABINETS BY

OPEN ELEVATIONS

JOB SITE ADDRESS

157 S. ORANGE AVE.
LOS ANGELES, CA. 90036

DRAWN BY: JOHN

DATE: 8 MAR 90

SCALE: 1/2" = 1'0"

REVISED: 1 4/12/90 2 4 5

SHEET NO. 5 OF 7

FOR THE RESIDENCE OF DON AND SALLY SILVERS
AT 157 S. ORANGE AVE
LOS ANGELES, CA 90036

APPROVED BY ___ DATE ___

D.E. SILVERS (213) 934-4761
137 NORTH DETROIT STREET
LOS ANGELES, CALIFORNIA 90036

THIS DRAWING IS THE EXCLUSIVE PROPERTY OF D.E. SILVERS

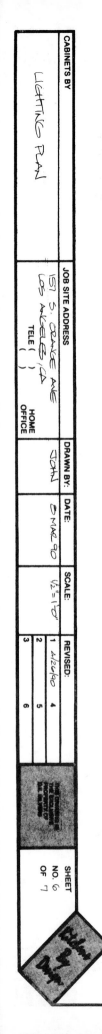

CABINETS BY

LIGHTING PLAN

JOB SITE ADDRESS

157 S. ORANGE AVE
LOS ANGELES, CA

TELE ( )
( )

HOME
OFFICE

DRAWN BY: JOHN

DATE: 8 MAR 90

SCALE: 1/2" = 1'-0"

REVISED:
1	4/20/90	4
2		5
3		6

SHEET
NO. 6
OF 7

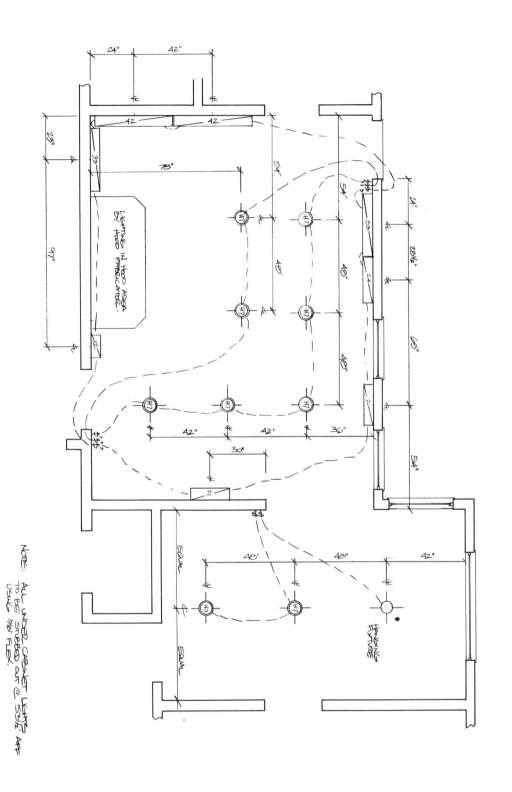

NOTE: ALL UNDER CABINET LIGHTS
TO BE STUBBED OUT @ 53½" AFF
USING ⅜" FLEX.

LIGHTING IN HOOD AREA
BY HOOD FABRICATOR.

HANGING FIXTURE

FOR THE RESIDENCE OF
AT
DON AND SALLY SILVERS
157 S ORANGE AVE
LOS ANGELES, CA 90036

APPROVED BY

DATE

D.E. SILVERS (213) 934-4761

137 NORTH DETROIT STREET
LOS ANGELES, CALIFORNIA 90036

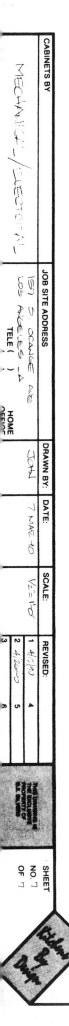

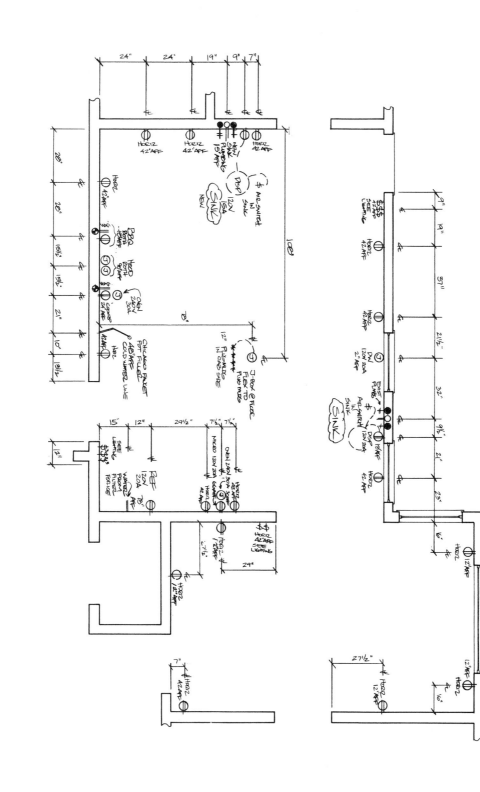

FOR THE RESIDENCE OF DON AND SALLY SILVERS
AT 151 S ORANGE AVE
LOS ANGELES, LA 90036

APPROVED BY   DATE

D.E. SILVERS   (213) 934-4761

137 NORTH DETROIT STREET
LOS ANGELES, CALIFORNIA 90036

YOUR KITCHEN QUESTIONNAIRE

The following survey should help you determine your needs—and answer the questions of any good kitchen designer you are thinking about working with. In fact, if the kitchen designer doesn't ask or care about these issues, keep looking!

1. How many eat at home on a daily basis?
Monday___ Tuesday___ Wednesday___ Thursday___ Friday___ Saturday___ Sunday___
Breakfast___ Lunch___ Dinner

2. How often—and for how many—do you entertain informally?
Weekly____ Bi-monthly____ Monthly____
1-3____ 4-6____ 7 or more____

3. What is a sample informal dinner menu?

_____

_____

4. What is a favorite entree you serve for an informal dinner?

_____

_____

5. How often—and for how many—do you entertain formally?
Weekly____ Bi-monthly____ Monthly____
1-3____ 4-6____ 7 or more____

6. When you cook formally, how many people help in the kitchen? _____

7. What is a sample formal dinner menu?

_____

_____

8. What is a favorite entree you serve for a formal dinner?

_____

_____

9. What is a sample menu you would prepare for the family?

_____

_____

10. Would you create any different menus with a new kitchen? _____

11. What appliance do you like to work with most? _____

12. What appliance do you like to work with least? _____

13. What appliance that you don't have would you most like? _____

14. Do you prefer to sit or stand while doing prep work? _____

15. Are you right- or left-handed?_____

16. Who in the family is the primary cook?_____

17. How tall is the primary cook? _____

18. Does the primary cook have any physical limitations?_____

19. What do you not like about your present kitchen?

_____

_____

20. What do you most like about your present kitchen?

_____

_____

21. What are the reasons you would want to change your kitchen?

_____

_____

22. Do you like to work in your kitchen alone, or have guests visiting with you or helping you while you cook? _____

23. What kind of access would you like your kitchen to have to adjacent rooms?

_____

_____

24. What type of feeling would you like your new kitchen to have?

Contemporary _____   Family Retreat _____

Open and Airy _____   Traditional _____

Warm and Cozy Country_____   Formal _____

Personal Design Statement _____

25. What colors do you like? _____

    Dislike? _____

26. Do you want to relocate or change doors, windows or walls?

_____

_____

27. Do you need an area in your kitchen to plan menus, store cookbooks or serve any other purpose?_____

28. How often do you grocery shop?

Daily_____   Bi-weekly_____   Weekly_____

29. What percentages of frozen, canned and fresh foods do you buy?

Frozen_____   Canned_____   Fresh_____

30. Do you have enough storage space? _____

31. How many sets of dishes or china do you have? _____

32. How many sets of glassware or crystal do you have? _____

33. How many sets of flatware or silverware do you have? _____

34. Do you have any other storage space for these items than in the kitchen?_____

35. Do you do any of the following?

Can_____   Make candy_____   Bake_____   Make pasta_____

Dehydrate food_____   Make ice cream_____   Make stock_____   Other_____

36. Do you, or do you want to, recycle any of the following?

Plastic_____   Clear glass_____   Green glass_____   Brown glass_____

Paper_____   Compact refuse_____   Other_____

37. Do you have, or would you like, a sorting station in any of these areas?

Kitchen_____   Garage_____   Utility room_____   Basement_____   Other_____

38. Do you have any of the following small wares? Do you store them on the counter or in a cabinet?

Blender _____

Bread machine _____

Can opener _____

Coffee grinder _____

Crepe maker _____

Crockpot _____

Deep-fat fryer _____

Dehydrator _____

Electric frying pan _____

Espresso machine _____

Food grinder _____

Food processor _____

Food slicer_____

Griddle _____

Hand mixer _____

Heavy mixer _____

Ice cream maker _____

Ice crusher_____

Immersion blender_____

Juicer_____

Knife sharpener_____

Pasta machine _____

Pizza stone _____

Popcorn maker _____

Sandwich maker _____

Scale _____

Steamer _____

Toaster_____

Toaster oven _____

Waffle maker_____

Wok_____

Yogurt maker_____

Other _____

39. Which, if any, of the following would you like in your kitchen?

Study area_____   Sewing area_____   Laundry area_____   Ironing board_____   Stereo_____

Computer_____   Television_____   Plants/herbs_____   Telephone_____

40. List every item in your kitchen, indicating its frequency of use and where it is stored.
Used daily=D   Used within the week=W   Used within the month=M   Used occasionally=O
Wall cabinet=WC   Laundry=L   Basement=B   Appliance garage=AG
Countertop=CT   Base cabinet=BC   Desk=DK   Tall cabinet=TC

Dishes—everyday _____

_____

_____

China _____

_____

_____

Glasses-everyday _____

_____

_____

Crystal _____

_____

_____

Flatware _____

_____

_____

Silverware _____

_____

_____

Pots _____

_____

Pans _____

_____

Trays _____

_____

Serving pieces _____

_____

Storage containers _____

_____

_____

Knives _____

_____

_____

Utensils _____

_____

_____

Baking pans _____

_____

_____

Other _____

_____

_____

41. Where do you currently store the following?

Boxed goods _____

Canned goods _____

Cleaning supplies _____

Linens _____

Laundry soaps_____

Non-refrigerated fruits and vegetables _____

Paper products_____

Pet food_____

Recyclable containers _____

Spices _____

Table appointments_____

Wrapping materials_____

Other _____

BOOKS AVAILABLE FROM NMI PUBLISHERS

BUYING RETAIL IS STUPID!
Where to Buy Everything at Giant Savings in Southern California
By Trisha King-Crumley, Deborah Newmark and Bonnie Cunningham
(498 pages, Third Edition...$16.95)

This best selling regional book includes over 2,100 stores and outlets where you can buy EVERYTHING from A to Z—antiques, appliances, building materials, electronics furniture, groceries, jewelry, luggage, musical instruments, pets, sporting goods, wallpaper... and much more—at savings from 20% to 80% off retail prices. Also includes 150 mail order discount businesses from which you can buy all the above at great savings.

HAPPINESS THROUGH SUPERFICIALITY
The War Against Meaningful Relationships
by Jerry Newmark and Irving S. Newmark
(176 pages, 1992...$11.95)

This book lifts your spirits, makes you laugh, challenges you to rethink your values and shows you how to lead a happier, more fulfilling life. The Doctors Newmark offer fresh perspectives, in a humorous and often provocative way, on many of the most serious aspects of life—sex, marriage, parenting, work, health, education, money, love, lawyers, doctors, psychotherapy and much more. You will learn how to stop taking everything too seriously—especially your self and how to come through the '90s whole and happy.

THIS SCHOOL BELONGS TO YOU & ME:
Every Learner A Teacher, Every Teacher A Learner
by Gerald Newmark
(431 pages, 1976...$9.95)

First published in 1976, this book remains an important resource for anyone interested in improving education. It describes a new kind of learning community—an exciting school where students, parents, teachers, staff and administrators are turned on to learning and to working cooperatively with each other.

"This School Belongs To You & Me" offers a detailed plan for the redesign of an entire school into a vibrant learning community. It is also a rich resource book of educational ideas and practices which can be used by individual teachers to improve and existing program or classroom. Developed from a seven-year, Ford Foundation supported project in inner-city elementary schools, the ideas presented can be applied to all school levels, whatever their geographic, ethnic, or soci-economic characteristics, in exciting, cost-effective ways.

To order any of the above books, send a check for the amount indicated, plus $3.00 for p&h (add $1 for each additional book) to: **NMI PUBLISHERS,** 18345 Ventura Blvd., Suite 314, Tarzana, CA 91356. For Credit Card orders call: 818-708-1244

If you would like additional copies of *The Complete Guide to Kitchen Design with Cooking in Mind* or are interested in the Consultation and Design Services of Donald E. Silvers, CKD, call him at: **800-900-4761.**

Write to: **Donald E. Silvers, KITCHEN & OTHER ENVIRONMENTS BY DESIGN,** 155 S. Orange Dr., Los Angeles, CA 90036.

New Ideas . . . from
a Century of Experience!

March 2, 1995

Mr. Don E. Silvers
155 South Orange Drive
Los Angeles, CA 90036

Dear Don,

You truly have been a life saver to me. I bought a home that had a kitchen designed by one of the better known kitchen designers in my city that made cooking a true chore. Thus, I decided to redo my kitchen. But, after going through two successive architects, I still didn't have a design that felt right. One Sunday, I came upon an article in our paper that simply said if you want to design your kitchen right you need the book on kitchen designs by Don Silvers. At that point, I was game for anything.

I sent for your book and found it extremely enlightening. Due to my hectic schedule and my loss of faith in the ability of architects designing kitchens, I asked and was pleasantly surprised, when you agreed to help me in my design. I truly feel comfortable with what you have done and can imagine stress free cooking in your wonderfully laid out kitchen that incorporated all of my needs and made the kitchen finally workable. I can't wait until the project is done.

I do want to thank you for all of your continual follow up and genuine interest in making sure this project comes out correctly. You sure have proven the axiom "don't believe everything you read in the paper", to be false.

Sincerely,

EAGLE CRUSHER COMPANY, INC.

Susanne Cobey
President/CEO

SC:rjg

4250 S.R. 309 • GALION, OHIO 44833 • FAX (419) 468-4840 • (419) 468-2288

Specializing in Self-Contained, Portable Crushing & Screening Plants for Recycle (Concrete, Asphalt, Rubble) and Hard Rock Crushing (Open Pit & Deep Mine)
Custom-Engineered Stationary and Portable Crushing Systems • Equipment & Parts (Eagle, Austin-Western, Diamond, Madsen, & Scoopmobile)

The Prudential

Pamela A. Bruning, CLU, ChFC
Managing Director

Buckeye Agency
Suite 170, 2600 Corporate Exchange Drive
Columbus, OH 43231-1670
Office: 614-895-3830 Ext. 1202
Fax: 614-895-3823

February 28, 1995

Donald Silvers, CKD
155 South Orange Drive
Los Angeles, CA 90036

Dear Don:

It is with a great deal of pleasure that I wish to take a few moments to thank you for your invaluable contributions to the "heart" of our new home - the kitchen.

It was pure chance that led me to read the newspaper that one Sunday (a luxury I usually don't have) and the article in it about you. After sending off for your book, reading it, and being very impressed with your ideas on REAL kitchens for people who REALLY cook, I decided to pursue utilization of your special talents.

I have been totally delighted with your ideas, your creativity, your responsiveness and your general professionalism. I have retained the series of drawings of our kitchen floor plan as they progressed from the initial architects rendering I sent to you to the final plan that is currently being built. It is amazing how much more functional and even more beautiful the space has become since you've been working on it. I was so frustrated initially with the plans submitted by our architect's and builder; here we were going to put all of this money into a house and I had a kitchen that did not "feel" right - and didn't know what to do about it!

Now I'm looking at the plans of the space I cannot wait to get into. The suggestions on design, on features, on layout and on over all work patterns of the space have been invaluable. The mere fact that you saved us from spending thousands of dollars on the wrong model commercial stove has repaid my initial investment in you many times over. Your suggestions on sources for cabinetry and interior options have resulted in a kitchen that will truly be a joy to work in.

Don, I don't know how many people in this country do what you do. I could wish there would be many, many more - as there would be many more families who would be as thrilled with their new homes as we will be. Until that happens, I can only hope that others like me, couples like Mac and I who are serious about our kitchens, have the good fortune to run into you. I wish you all the best in the future - may your business grow and prosper. If I ever build another home, rest assured that I will locate you, wherever you are, before I even begin to think about a builder.

Sincerely,

Pam

Pamela A. Bruning, CLU, ChFC

Registered Representative, Pruco Securities Corporation
A Subsidiary of The Prudential
1111 Durham Avenue, South Plainfield, NJ 07080
1-800-382-7121

HE SEALE ORGANIZATION

280 Camino Sur
Palm Springs, CA 92262
(760) 325-3519
Fax (760) 320-0610

March 12, 1998

Donald E. Silvers, CKD
155 South Orange Drive
Los Angeles, CA 90036

Dear Don:

Our new functional kitchen you designed is finished. It is incredibly beautiful, proving that you can have the best of both worlds. Thank you for designing it and walking me through all the steps. With your expertise, we achieved a result even better than anticipated within budget without compromising on anything.

Having been in the design and remodeling business, I have renovated many kitchens, replacing what the builder did. When it came to designing my own kitchen from scratch, I did not know where to begin. Fortunately I read your book *Kitchen Design With Cooking In Mind*. While I learned a lot from your book, I realized with the money I intended to spend, I wanted you to design it. Without your expertise, costly mistakes, far in excess of your fees, would have been made.

With your expertise, design and contacts, we were able to produce a "world class" kitchen more economically than would have been possible had I tried to "wing it alone". Many people take the "do it yourself" approach with a new kitchen because they think a certified kitchen designer is expensive. Not so! He who designs it himself, in my opinion, is a fool – even if he has design experience! Kitchen design is a specialty.

What sets you apart from other kitchen designers is your seasoned experience as a professional chef. Everything you put in the plan was logical and had a purpose for being there. Your advice on cabinet and appliance selection is invaluable.

Enclosed are some print outs of digital photographs. After decorative accessories are in, it will be professionally photographed, should you wish to use it in your new book.

Many thanks to you, my friend, for a project well done!

Sincerely,

Robert M. Seale

PLEASE SEND ME MY OWN COPY OF *KITCHEN DESIGN WITH COOKING IN MIND.*

Name _____

Address _____

City _____ State _____ Zip _____

Please send check or money order to:
Kitchens & Other Environments by Design, 155 S. Orange Drive, Los Angeles, California 90036

Or charge on MasterCard or Visa:

Card #_____ Exp. Date _____

If you would like additional information on our Design Assurance Program, or our design services, please call Don Silvers at **(800) 900-4761**.	**Book Total ($24.95 ea.)** _____ **Shipping & Handling (4.00 ea.)** _____ **Sales Tax (CA only - $2.06 ea.)** _____ **Order Total** _____

- -

PLEASE SEND ME MY OWN COPY OF *KITCHEN DESIGN WITH COOKING IN MIND.*

Name _____

Address _____

City _____ State _____ Zip _____

Please send check or money order to:
Kitchens & Other Environments by Design, 155 S. Orange Drive, Los Angeles, California 90036

Or charge on MasterCard or Visa:

Card #_____ Exp. Date _____

If you would like additional information on our Design Assurance Program, or our design services, please call Don Silvers at **(800) 900-4761**.	**Book Total ($24.95 ea.)** _____ **Shipping & Handling (4.00 ea.)** _____ **Sales Tax (CA only - $2.06 ea.)** _____ **Order Total** _____

- -

PLEASE SEND ME MY OWN COPY OF *KITCHEN DESIGN WITH COOKING IN MIND.*

Name _____

Address _____

City _____ State _____ Zip _____

Please send check or money order to:
Kitchens & Other Environments by Design, 155 S. Orange Drive, Los Angeles, California 90036

Or charge on MasterCard or Visa:

Card #_____ Exp. Date _____

If you would like additional information on our Design Assurance Program, or our design services, please call Don Silvers at **(800) 900-4761**.	**Book Total ($24.95 ea.)** _____ **Shipping & Handling (4.00 ea.)** _____ **Sales Tax (CA only - $2.06 ea.)** _____ **Order Total** _____

PDR® 2010 EDITION
NURSE'S DRUG HANDBOOK

W9-BGF-938

THE INFORMATION STANDARD FOR
PRESCRIPTION DRUGS AND
NURSING CONSIDERATIONS